CHEFMAN
Digital Air Fryer

COOKBOOK

for Beginners

Crispy, Healthy & Delicious
Recipes for Your Chefman Air
Fryer to Air Fry, Bake, Roast,
Rotisserie and Dehydrate (Full
Color Edition)

Larry Galiano

Table of Content

INTRODUCTION

Welcome to the inspiring world of the CHEFMAN Multifunctional Digital Air Fryer+, a gem that has redefined my personal cooking experience and promises to transform yours. As your guide and fellow culinary explorer, I invite you to join me in discovering the elegance and versatility of this extraordinary kitchen companion.

The CHEFMAN Air Fryer+ is not merely an air fryer; it is a masterful blend of a rotisserie, dehydrator, and convection oven, all integrated into one sleek unit with a large 10-liter capacity. This allows for not only family-sized meals but also the ability to entertain guests with restaurant-quality dishes, all made in the comfort of your home. The large easy-view window has been a personal revelation, allowing me to watch my dishes blossom in real-time without ever lifting the lid, maintaining the perfect cooking environment.

With 17 digital touch screen presets, this air fryer eliminates guesswork from cooking. Each feature is designed to bring out the best in your ingredients, whether you are air frying potatoes to a perfect golden crisp or roasting a chicken that emerges succulently moist inside with a beautifully crisp exterior. My personal favorite is the dehydrator function; it has allowed me to make incredible homemade snacks like apple chips and beef jerky with ease.

Safety and convenience are paramount with the CHEFMAN Air Fryer+. The auto shutoff function ensures the appliance never overheats, giving me peace of mind whenever I'm multitasking in the kitchen. This thoughtful feature, along with the energy-efficient design, exemplifies how the CHEFMAN Air Fryer+ respects both your safety and your time.

In this cookbook, you will find recipes that I have carefully developed and tested, each tailored to leverage the CHEFMAN Air Fryer+'s capabilities. From quick family dinners to elaborate party appetizers, these recipes will guide you through a plethora of flavors and techniques that make the most of this appliance. My hope is that through these pages, you will discover not just the joy of cooking, but the joy of cooking smarter, faster, and healthier.

Let the CHEFMAN Multifunctional Digital Air Fryer+ inspire you as it has inspired me, transforming everyday cooking into a delightful culinary adventure. Welcome to a new era of home cooking, where every meal is a celebration of taste and technology.

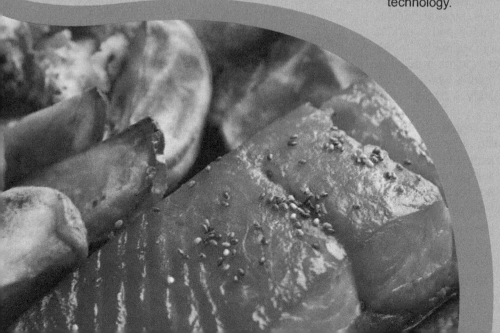

CHAPTER 1

Getting Started with Your CHEFMAN Air Fryer+

The CHEFMAN Multifunctional Digital Air Fryer+ is a cutting-edge appliance that brings versatility and convenience into the modern kitchen. Designed to cater to a variety of cooking needs, this air fryer enables you to bake, roast, dehydrate, and air fry with minimal effort and maximum efficiency. Its sleek design integrates smoothly into any kitchen aesthetic, providing both functionality and style.

One of the standout features of this air fryer is its capacitive touch control panel, which offers a user-friendly interface for easy operation. The panel includes options for different cooking methods and presets for popular dishes, ensuring that every meal is just a touch away. Whether you're preparing crispy fries, a juicy roast, or dehydrated fruits, the CHEFMAN Air Fryer+ makes the process simple and enjoyable.

Safety is a key component of the CHEFMAN Air Fryer+'s design. It includes several built-in safety features such as auto-shutoff and overheat protection, which help prevent accidents in the kitchen. This attention to safety makes it suitable for families and even novice cooks who may be unfamiliar with air frying technology.

The CHEFMAN Multifunctional Digital Air Fryer+ also emphasizes efficiency. With its quick heating capability, you can cook meals faster than traditional ovens and without the need for preheating. This not only saves time but also reduces energy consumption, making it an eco-friendlier choice for meal preparation.

In summary, the CHEFMAN Multifunctional Digital Air Fryer+ is more than just an appliance; it's a versatile partner in the kitchen that helps you create a variety of dishes quickly and safely. Its combination of advanced features, safety measures, and efficient performance makes it an essential tool for any modern cook looking to simplify their cooking routine.

Benefits of CHEFMAN Multifunctional Air Fryer+

The CHEFMAN Multifunctional Digital Air Fryer+ offers a plethora of benefits that make it a standout choice for home cooks seeking versatility, convenience, and healthier cooking options. Here are the key advantages that users can enjoy with this innovative appliance:

- **Healthier Cooking Options**
The CHEFMAN Air Fryer+ drastically reduces the amount of oil needed for frying, allowing you to prepare your favorite dishes with fewer calories and less fat. This feature is crucial for those looking to maintain a healthier lifestyle without sacrificing taste.

- **Versatile Cooking Functions**
With functions to air fry, bake, roast, and dehydrate, this air fryer caters to a broad range of cooking needs. Each mode is optimized to deliver perfect results, whether you're making crispy snacks, tender roasts, or preserving fruits and vegetables.

- **Convenience and User-Friendly Interface**
The air fryer features a capacitive touch control panel that simplifies the cooking process. Pre-set cooking modes make it easy to start meals quickly, and the appliance's straightforward design ensures that cleaning up is just as easy as setting up.

- **Time Efficiency**
This air fryer heats up quickly and cooks food faster than conventional ovens. The quick cooking time, coupled with no need for preheating, helps save time and energy, making meal preparation more efficient.

- **Safety Features**
Built with safety in mind, the CHEFMAN Air Fryer+ includes features like auto-shutoff and overheat protection to ensure safe operation every time. These features help prevent common cooking accidents, providing peace of mind for all users.

- **Compact and Sleek Design**
The air fryer's compact design makes it suitable for any kitchen size, saving valuable countertop space. Its modern aesthetic complements any kitchen décor, ensuring that it looks good while being highly functional.

- **Energy Efficiency**
By cooking more quickly and requiring no preheating, the air fryer reduces overall energy consumption compared to traditional cooking methods. This efficiency is not only good for the environment but also helps lower household energy bills.

- **Enhanced Flavor and Texture**
The air fryer's advanced technology ensures that foods not only cook quickly but also come out crispy on the outside and tender on the inside, enhancing both the flavor and texture of your meals.

These benefits highlight the CHEFMAN Multifunctional Digital Air Fryer+'s ability to transform kitchen routines, offering a blend of health, efficiency, and culinary excellence that is well-suited to today's busy lifestyles.

Understanding the Control Panel

The control panel of the CHEFMAN Multifunctional Digital Air Fryer+ is streamlined and user-friendly, providing intuitive access to a range of functions that enhance cooking versatility. Below is a detailed explanation of each component and its function:

1. Temperature/Cook Time Display
This display alternates between showing the current temperature and the remaining cook time, keeping you informed of essential cooking parameters without manual input.

2. Cooking Functions
BAKE, AIR FRY, DEHYDRATE: Choose your desired cooking mode with these dedicated buttons. Each function is optimized for specific types of cooking, ensuring you get the best results whether you're baking cakes, air frying chicken, or dehydrating fruits.

3. Cooking Presets
The air fryer includes several presets that automatically adjust the temperature and time settings for commonly cooked foods, enhancing ease of use and ensuring consistent results:
- ◊ Cake
- ◊ Fries
- ◊ Chicken
- ◊ Fish
- ◊ Meat
- ◊ Vegetables
- ◊ Fruit

These presets simplify the cooking process, making it easier to prepare these items with just a few button presses.

4. ROTATE
Activates the rotisserie function, ideal for even cooking of rotisserie chickens or other meats by rotating them during the cooking process.

5. LIGHT
Illuminates the interior of the air fryer, allowing you to visually monitor your food's progress without opening the door.

6. TEMP/TIME Toggle
This button switches between setting the temperature and adjusting the cooking timer, facilitating precise control over how your food is cooked.

7. Plus and Minus Signs
Use these buttons to increase or decrease the temperature and timer settings. The adjustments are straightforward, helping you fine-tune cooking conditions to your exact preference.

8. START
Initiates the cooking process with the chosen settings. Once pressed, the air fryer will begin to cook according to the selected function and adjustments.

9. STOP/CANCEL
This safety feature immediately ceases the cooking process. It is essential for quickly stopping the air fryer if you need to interrupt cooking for any reason.

Familiarizing yourself with these controls on your CHEFMAN Multifunctional Digital Air Fryer+ will make your culinary efforts more efficient and enjoyable, allowing you to easily prepare a variety of dishes with precision and confidence.

How to Use the Air Fryer

Using your CHEFMAN Multifunctional Digital Air Fryer+ is straightforward and can greatly enhance your cooking experience. Here's a step-by-step guide to help you get started:

1. Setup
Place the air fryer on a flat, stable surface away from any sources of heat and water. Ensure the area is well-ventilated. Plug in the air fryer to power it on.

2. Prepare for Cooking
If you are not using the drip tray for baking, position it at the bottom of the unit to facilitate easy cleaning later.

3. Loading the Air Fryer
Place your seasoned food on the appropriate accessory, whether it's the rack(s), baking pan, or spit. For directions on using the spit, refer to the corresponding rotisserie spit section.

4. Positioning Inside the Air Fryer

Insert the loaded rack(s), pan, or spit into the air fryer and securely close the door.

5. Selecting the Cooking Function
Choose your desired cooking function (BAKE, AIR FRY, or DEHYDRATE) by pressing the respective button on the control panel. The selected function will illuminate in blue, and food icons related to the function will appear on the panel. The device defaults to Air Fry when initially turned on.

6. Adjusting Settings
If utilizing the cooking presets, select the icon that matches the food you are cooking. This action sets the recommended temperature and time, which will display on the control panel. You can customize these by pressing the TEMP/TIME button and then using the plus and minus buttons to adjust as needed. Always check your food for doneness as per the food safety guidelines, rather than relying solely on preset times and temperatures.

7. Starting the Cooking Process
Press the START button to begin cooking. The button will turn red, the fan will activate, and the air fryer will start operating. You can monitor your cooking progress by pressing the LIGHT button to illuminate the interior or by opening the door; doing so will pause the cooking, but the air fryer will resume with the saved settings once the door is closed again. The STOP/CANCEL button can be pressed at any time to halt cooking.

8. Using the Rotisserie Spit
If you're using the spit, remember to press the ROTATE button to ensure the food is cooked evenly. This function does not activate automatically and can be turned on or off during cooking.

9. Completion

The air fryer will alert you with a beep and turn off automatically once the timer ends. Always check that your food is thoroughly cooked according to food safety guidelines before serving. Additional cooking time can be added if necessary.

10. Removing the Food
Carefully remove the hot food using potholders or oven mitts. If you used the spit, employ the fetch tool and an oven mitt to safely remove it.

11. Serving
Transfer the hot contents to a heat-resistant surface. Use tongs to handle and serve your delicious, freshly air-fried foods.

12. Safety Note
This appliance cooks with hot air; never attempt to heat a cooking vessel filled with oil or any other liquid inside the air fryer as this poses a serious fire hazard or risk of personal injury.

By following these steps, you can enjoy a variety of dishes prepared quickly and safely using your CHEFMAN Multifunctional Digital Air Fryer+.

How to Use the Rotisserie Spit

The rotisserie spit feature of the CHEFMAN Multifunctional Digital Air Fryer+ allows for even roasting and is perfect for a variety of foods including whole chickens, boneless pieces of meat, and even vegetables like cauliflower or fruits such as pineapple. Here's how to use the rotisserie spit effectively:

> Preparation of the Unit
Ensure that the drip tray is correctly placed at the bottom of the unit. This will catch any drips and make cleaning easier after cooking.

> Preparing the Food
For Whole Chicken: Remove giblets and season the chicken as desired. Truss the chicken tightly to ensure it cooks evenly. The chicken should fit comfortably in the oven with enough room to rotate—typically, a chicken weighing between 3 to 3½ pounds is ideal. Insert the spit through the length of the chicken, starting at the cavity. Attach the spit forks onto the shaft at both ends, embedding them deeply into the meat to secure the chicken. Ensure there is at least 1 inch of free space on each end of the spit rod.

For Meats: Slide the spit lengthwise through the center of the meat, such as beef or pork tenderloins. Attach the spit forks at both ends, ensuring they penetrate deeply and are locked in place with the screws, providing stability during rotation.

> Installing the Spit in the Air Fryer
Place the left end of the spit into the rotisserie gear inside the left wall of the air fryer. Then, carefully position the right end on the rotisserie holder on the right wall. Make sure the spit is secure and that the food has enough clearance to rotate freely without obstruction. Close the air fryer door to maintain the internal temperature and ensure safe operation.

> Cooking Process
Choose either the Bake or Air Fry function to start cooking. Follow the specific instructions on the control panel to select the correct settings for your dish. Remember, the spit will become very hot during cooking; always handle it with care.

> Using the Fetch Tool
To safely remove the hot spit after cooking, use the fetch tool. Hold the tool by its handle with one hand and place a potholder or oven mitt on the other hand for protection. Insert the fetch tool under the rotisserie spit and carefully lift the right side first, then the left, to free the spit from its holders.

> **Post-Cooking Handling**

Carefully guide the hot spit out of the air fryer and transfer it to a heat-resistant surface. Be cautious as the spit and the food will be very hot.

Mastering the use of the rotisserie spit in the CHEFMAN Multifunctional Digital Air Fryer+ is straightforward with this guide, allowing you to enjoy perfectly roasted meals with ease. Always exercise caution when handling the spit and other hot components to maintain a safe cooking environment.

Air Fryer Cooking Tips

Here are some useful tips for achieving the best results when cooking with the CHEFMAN Multifunctional Digital Air Fryer+:

■ **Preparation of Foods**

Minimal Oil Needed: Most prepared foods do not require additional oil before air frying. Foods that typically contain oil or other ingredients that aid in browning and crispiness, such as frozen appetizers or hors d'oeuvres, will air fry very well on their own. Tossing with Oil: For foods you prepare from scratch, like fresh french fries, tossing them lightly with oil in a separate bowl before cooking can enhance browning and crispiness.

■ **Dealing with Moisture**

Drying Foods: When making french fries from fresh potatoes, make sure the potatoes are completely dry before air frying. Even small amounts of moisture can prevent the fries from becoming crispy.

■ **Battered Foods**

Batter Consistency: When air frying foods with batter, use thicker, pasty batters rather than thin, runny batters. Thin batters, like those used for making tempura, will not set quickly enough and will run off the food, unlike in deep frying where they set immediately.

■ **Rack Management**

Multiple Racks: If using multiple wire racks during cooking, it's beneficial to switch the rack positions halfway through the cooking cycle. This ensures the most even cooking results, especially when air frying multiple layers of food.

■ **Reheating Food**

Optimal Temperature: The air fryer is excellent for reheating food. To reheat, set the temperature to 300°F and heat for up to 10 minutes to restore the food's warmth and crispness effectively.

■ **Food Safety**

Checking Doneness: Follow food safety guidelines for doneness. Since food sizes and thicknesses can vary significantly, use a food thermometer to ensure foods reach safe internal temperatures, rather than relying solely on cooking times provided by recipes.

These tips will help you maximize the use of your CHEFMAN Multifunctional Digital Air Fryer+, allowing you to enjoy delicious, crispy, and perfectly cooked meals every time.

Cleaning and Maintenance

Maintaining your CHEFMAN Multifunctional Digital Air Fryer+ properly ensures it continues to perform well and last longer. Here are the recommended steps for effective cleaning:

√ **Cool Down**

Before cleaning, unplug the air fryer and allow it to cool completely. This is crucial to ensure safety and prevent damage.

√ **Wipe Down**

Use a damp cloth or paper towel to gently clean the exterior and interior surfaces of the air fryer. Ensure the appliance, including its plug, is never immersed in water or any other liquid. The housing is not dishwasher safe and should be handled accordingly.

√ **Door Cleaning**

To clean the glass on the door, use a sponge, soft cloth, or nylon pad with dish soap and warm water. Make sure to dry the glass thoroughly after washing to avoid streaks. Avoid using spray glass cleaners. For easier access, the door can be removed: open it slightly and gently lift it upwards until it releases from the notches in the hinges. To reattach, hold the door upright, align the hinges, and gently push it down until it snaps back into place.

√ Accessory Care
Clean any removable accessories, such as the racks, with a sponge and warm, soapy water. If necessary, a bristled brush can be used to scrub away food residue. Avoid abrasive cleaners and scouring pads that could damage the surfaces. These accessories are safe for cleaning on the top rack of the dishwasher.

√ Drying and Storage
After cleaning, make sure to dry the unit and all accessories completely. Store the air fryer and its components in a cool, dry place to prevent any moisture buildup or damage.

Regular upkeep of your CHEFMAN Multifunctional Digital Air Fryer+ will ensure that it remains a reliable tool in your kitchen, ready to assist in making healthy and delicious meals. Proper care and storage help maintain the quality and safety of the appliance.

Troubleshooting and FAQs

When using your CHEFMAN Multifunctional Digital Air Fryer+, you may encounter some common issues. Below are some frequently asked questions and their solutions to help you quickly resolve these issues and ensure optimal performance of your air fryer.

1. Why is there white smoke coming from my unit?
Cause: White smoke often indicates that there is too much fat content within the air fryer. This can happen when cooking very fatty foods such as sausages.
Solution: Try to avoid cooking overly fatty foods, and always ensure that the air fryer and its accessories are clean before starting your cooking process.

CAUTION: If you notice black smoke emanating from the unit, this signifies a more severe problem, such as an electrical fault.
Immediate Action: Unplug the air fryer immediately, do not use it further, and contact Chefman Customer Support for assistance.

2. Why has my food cooked unevenly?
Common Causes: Uneven cooking can result from overcrowding the cooking basket or not switching the positions of the racks during the cooking process.
Solution: Ensure that food is evenly distributed on the racks and not overcrowded. During cooking, flipping the food or switching the rack positions at least once can help achieve more uniform cooking results.

3. Why isn't my food crisp?
Potential Issue: While the air fryer can cook with no added oil, not using enough oil can affect the crispiness of the food.
Solution: For optimal crispiness, lightly coat your food with oil—typically just a half teaspoon per batch is sufficient. This small amount of oil will help achieve the desired crisp texture.

4. Why is the unit displaying an error code?
Error Codes (E1 or E2): These codes indicate a technical problem with the air fryer, such as a short circuit.
Recommended Action: If these error codes appear, stop using the unit and contact Chefman Customer Support for guidance on a possible replacement or repair.

Understanding these common issues and knowing how to address them will help maintain the functionality and longevity of your CHEFMAN Multifunctional Digital Air Fryer+. For any persistent issues or questions, contacting customer support is always a recommended practice to ensure safe and efficient operation of your appliance.

CHAPTER 2

Breakfast

French Toast Sticks

Serves: 4

4 slices of thick bread
2 eggs
½ cup milk
1 tsp. vanilla extract
1 tsp. ground cinnamon
2 tbsps. sugar
2 tbsps. melted butter

|PREP TIME: 10 minutes
|COOK TIME: 10 minutes

1. Cut each slice of bread into 4 sticks.
2. In a shallow bowl, whisk together the eggs, milk, vanilla extract, and ground cinnamon.
3. Dip each bread stick into the egg mixture, ensuring it is fully coated.
4. Lightly grease two wire racks with melted butter.
5. Arrange the French toast sticks on the wire racks in a single layer, ensuring they do not overlap.
6. Position the drip tray on the floor of the unit for easy cleaning.
7. Insert the wire racks into the Air Fryer. Close the door.
8. Select the AIR FRY function, set the temperature to 375°F, and the time to 10 minutes. Press the START button to begin cooking.
9. Halfway through the cooking time, flip the French toast sticks to ensure even cooking.
10. Once the French toast sticks are golden brown and crispy, remove them from the Air Fryer.
11. Serve warm with maple syrup or powdered sugar.

Homemade Blueberry Muffins

Serves: 6

1½ cups all-purpose flour
½ cup sugar
2 tsps. baking powder
½ tsp. salt
½ cup milk
¼ cup vegetable oil
1 egg
1 tsp. vanilla extract
1 cup fresh or frozen blueberries

|PREP TIME: 10 minutes
|COOK TIME: 18 minutes

1. In a large bowl, whisk together the flour, sugar, baking powder, and salt.
2. In another bowl, mix together the milk, vegetable oil, egg, and vanilla extract.
3. Pour the wet ingredients into the dry ingredients and mix until just combined.
4. Gently fold in the blueberries.
5. Lightly grease a muffin pan that fits into your air fryer.
6. Divide the batter evenly among the muffin cups.
7. Place the muffin pan on the drip tray and insert the tray into the Air Fryer. Close the door.
8. Select the BAKE function, set the temperature to 350°F, and the time to 18 minutes. Press the START button to begin cooking.
9. Cook until the muffins are golden brown and a toothpick inserted into the center comes out clean.
10. Serve warm.

Breakfast Sausage

|PREP TIME: 10 minutes
|COOK TIME: 10 minutes

1 lb. ground pork
1 tsp. salt
½ tsp. black pepper
½ tsp. garlic powder
½ tsp. onion powder
½ tsp. smoked paprika
½ tsp. dried sage
¼ tsp. dried thyme
¼ tsp. crushed red pepper flakes (optional)

1. In a large bowl, combine the ground pork with all the seasonings: salt, black pepper, garlic powder, onion powder, smoked paprika, dried sage, dried thyme, and crushed red pepper flakes.
2. Mix well until the seasonings are evenly distributed throughout the meat.
3. Form the seasoned pork mixture into 12 small sausage patties.
4. Lightly grease two wire racks.
5. Arrange the sausage patties on the wire racks in a single layer, ensuring they do not overlap.
6. Position the drip tray on the floor of the unit for easy cleaning.
7. Insert the wire racks into the Air Fryer. Close the door.
8. Select the AIR FRY function, set the temperature to 375°F, and the time to 10 minutes. Press the START button to begin cooking.
9. Halfway through the cooking time, switch the rack positions from top to bottom to ensure even cooking.
10. Once the sausages are cooked through and golden brown, remove them from the Air Fryer.
11. Serve warm.

Hash Browns

|PREP TIME: 10 minutes
|COOK TIME: 15 minutes

4 medium potatoes, peeled and shredded
1 small onion, finely chopped
1 egg
2 tbsps. flour
1 tsp. salt
½ tsp. black pepper

1. In a large bowl, combine the shredded potatoes, chopped onion, egg, flour, salt, and black pepper. Mix well.
2. Lightly grease two wire racks.
3. Form the potato mixture into small patties and place them on the wire racks in a single layer, ensuring they do not overlap.
4. Position the drip tray on the floor of the unit for easy cleaning.
5. Insert the wire racks into the Air Fryer. Close the door.
6. Select the AIR FRY function, set the temperature to 390°F, and the time to 15 minutes. Press the START button to begin cooking.
7. Halfway through the cooking time, switch the rack positions from top to bottom to ensure even cooking.
8. Once the hash browns are golden brown and crispy, remove them from the Air Fryer.
9. Serve warm.

Simple Cinnamon Rolls

Serves: 8

1 can (8 count) refrigerated cinnamon rolls with icing

|PREP TIME: 15 minutes
|COOK TIME: 15 minutes

1. Open the can of refrigerated cinnamon rolls and separate them.
2. Lightly grease two wire racks.
3. Arrange the cinnamon rolls on the wire racks in a single layer, ensuring they do not overlap.
4. Position the drip tray on the floor of the unit for easy cleaning.
5. Insert the wire racks into the Air Fryer. Close the door.
6. Select the BAKE function, set the temperature to 350°F, and the time to 15 minutes. Press the START button to begin cooking.
7. Halfway through the cooking time, switch the rack positions from top to bottom to ensure even cooking.
8. Once the cinnamon rolls are golden brown, remove them from the Air Fryer.
9. Drizzle the icing over the warm cinnamon rolls.
10. Serve warm.

Breakfast Burritos

Serves: 4

4 large flour tortillas
4 eggs
½ cup shredded cheddar cheese
½ cup cooked breakfast sausage, crumbled

¼ cup diced bell peppers
¼ cup diced onions
Salt and pepper to taste
Salsa and sour cream for serving

|PREP TIME: 15 minutes
|COOK TIME: 10 minutes

1. In a skillet over medium heat, cook the diced bell peppers and onions until softened.
2. Add the crumbled breakfast sausage to the skillet and cook until heated through.
3. In a separate bowl, whisk the eggs with salt and pepper. Scramble the eggs in the skillet until fully cooked.
4. Warm the flour tortillas in the microwave for about 20 seconds to make them more pliable.
5. Divide the scrambled eggs, sausage mixture, and shredded cheddar cheese evenly among the tortillas.
6. Roll up each tortilla to form a burrito, folding in the sides to enclose the filling.
7. Lightly grease one wire rack.
8. Place the burritos on the wire rack, ensuring they do not overlap.
9. Position the drip tray on the floor of the unit for easy cleaning.
10. Insert the wire rack into the Air Fryer. Close the door.
11. Select the AIR FRY function, set the temperature to 350°F, and the time to 10 minutes. Press the START button to begin cooking.
12. Once the burritos are golden brown and crispy, remove them from the Air Fryer.
13. Serve warm with salsa and sour cream.

Healthy Avocado Toast

Serves: 4

|PREP TIME: 5 minutes
|COOK TIME: 5 minutes

4 slices of whole grain bread
2 ripe avocados
1 tbsp. lemon juice
Salt and pepper to taste
Optional toppings: cherry tomatoes, red pepper flakes, olive oil

1. Lightly grease one wire rack.
2. Arrange the slices of bread on the wire rack in a single layer.
3. Position the drip tray on the floor of the unit for easy cleaning.
4. Insert the wire rack into the Air Fryer. Close the door.
5. Select the AIR FRY function, set the temperature to 400°F, and the time to 5 minutes. Press the START button to begin cooking.
6. While the bread is toasting, mash the avocados in a bowl and mix in the lemon juice, salt, and pepper.
7. Once the toast is golden brown, remove it from the Air Fryer.
8. Spread the mashed avocado mixture evenly over each slice of toast.
9. Add optional toppings if desired.
10. Serve immediately.

Apple Fritters

Serves: 6

|PREP TIME: 15 minutes
|COOK TIME: 12 minutes

1 cup all-purpose flour
¼ cup sugar
1 tsp. baking powder
½ tsp. ground cinnamon
¼ tsp. salt
½ cup milk
1 egg
1 tsp. vanilla extract
1 large apple, peeled, cored, and diced
Powdered sugar for dusting

1. In a large bowl, whisk together the flour, sugar, baking powder, cinnamon, and salt.
2. In another bowl, mix together the milk, egg, and vanilla extract.
3. Pour the wet ingredients into the dry ingredients and mix until just combined.
4. Fold in the diced apple.
5. Lightly grease two wire racks.
6. Drop spoonfuls of the batter onto the wire racks, forming small fritters.
7. Position the drip tray on the floor of the unit for easy cleaning.
8. Insert the wire racks into the Air Fryer. Close the door.
9. Select the AIR FRY function, set the temperature to 350°F, and the time to 12 minutes. Press the START button to begin cooking.
10. Halfway through the cooking time, switch the rack positions from top to bottom to ensure even cooking.
11. Once the fritters are golden brown, remove them from the Air Fryer.
12. Dust with powdered sugar and serve warm.

Breakfast Casserole

6 large eggs
½ cup milk
½ cup cooked breakfast sausage, crumbled
½ cup diced bell peppers
¼ cup diced onions
1 cup shredded cheddar cheese
Salt and pepper to taste

|PREP TIME: 15 minutes
|COOK TIME: 25 minutes

1. In a large bowl, whisk together the eggs, milk, salt, and pepper.
2. Stir in the cooked sausage, bell peppers, onions, and half of the shredded cheese.
3. Lightly grease a baking dish that fits into your air fryer.
4. Pour the mixture into the prepared baking dish.
5. Sprinkle the remaining cheese on top.
6. Place the baking dish on the drip tray and insert the tray into the Air Fryer. Close the door.
7. Select the BAKE function, set the temperature to 350°F, and the time to 25 minutes. Press the START button to begin cooking.
8. Cook until the casserole is set and the cheese is melted and golden brown.
9. Serve warm.

Ham and Pepper Muffins

6 large eggs
¼ cup milk
½ cup diced bell peppers
½ cup diced ham
¼ cup shredded cheddar cheese
Salt and pepper to taste

|PREP TIME: 10 minutes
|COOK TIME: 12 minutes

1. In a large bowl, whisk together the eggs, milk, salt, and pepper.
2. Stir in the diced bell peppers, diced ham, and shredded cheddar cheese.
3. Lightly grease a muffin pan that fits into your air fryer.
4. Pour the egg mixture evenly into the muffin cups.
5. Place the muffin pan on the drip tray and insert the tray into the Air Fryer. Close the door.
6. Select the BAKE function, set the temperature to 350°F, and the time to 12 minutes. Press the START button to begin cooking.
7. Cook until the egg muffins are set and a toothpick inserted into the center comes out clean.
8. Serve warm.

Chocolate Chip Banana Bread

Serves: 8

|PREP TIME: 15 minutes
|COOK TIME: 25 minutes

2 cups all-purpose flour
1 tsp. baking soda
¼ tsp. salt
½ cup unsalted butter, melted
¾ cup brown sugar
2 large eggs
1 tsp. vanilla extract
3 ripe bananas, mashed
1 cup chocolate chips

1. In a large bowl, whisk together the flour, baking soda, and salt.
2. In another bowl, mix together the melted butter, brown sugar, eggs, and vanilla extract until smooth.
3. Stir in the mashed bananas.
4. Gradually add the dry ingredients to the wet ingredients and mix until just combined.
5. Fold in the chocolate chips.
6. Lightly grease a loaf pan that fits into your air fryer.
7. Pour the batter into the prepared loaf pan.
8. Place the loaf pan on the drip tray and insert the tray into the Air Fryer. Close the door.
9. Select the BAKE function, set the temperature to 325°F, and the time to 25 minutes. Press the START button to begin cooking.
10. Cook until a toothpick inserted into the center comes out clean.
11. Let the banana bread cool slightly before slicing.
12. Serve warm or at room temperature.

Breakfast Potatoes

Serves: 4

|PREP TIME: 10 minutes
|COOK TIME: 20 minutes

4 medium potatoes, diced
¼ cup olive oil
1 tsp. garlic powder
1 tsp. paprika
½ tsp. salt
½ tsp. black pepper
¼ cup chopped fresh parsley (optional)

1. In a large bowl, toss the diced potatoes with olive oil, garlic powder, paprika, salt, and black pepper until evenly coated.
2. Lightly grease two wire racks.
3. Spread the potatoes evenly on the wire racks in a single layer.
4. Position the drip tray on the floor of the unit for easy cleaning.
5. Insert the wire racks into the Air Fryer. Close the door.
6. Select the AIR FRY function, set the temperature to 400°F, and the time to 20 minutes. Press the START button to begin cooking.
7. Halfway through the cooking time, switch the rack positions from top to bottom to ensure even cooking.
8. Once the potatoes are golden brown and crispy, remove them from the Air Fryer.
9. Sprinkle with chopped fresh parsley, if desired, and serve warm.

CHAPTER 3
Fish and Seafood

Lemon Garlic Shrimp

|PREP TIME: 10 minutes
|COOK TIME: 8 minutes

1 lb. large shrimp, peeled and deveined
2 tbsps. olive oil
2 cloves garlic, minced
1 lemon, juiced
½ tsp. salt
¼ tsp. black pepper
1 tbsp. chopped fresh parsley

1. In a large bowl, toss the shrimp with olive oil, minced garlic, lemon juice, salt, and black pepper until evenly coated.
2. Lightly grease one wire rack.
3. Arrange the shrimp on the wire rack in a single layer.
4. Position the drip tray on the floor of the unit for easy cleaning.
5. Insert the wire rack into the Air Fryer. Close the door.
6. Select the AIR FRY function, choose the FISH icon, set the temperature to 400°F, and the time to 8 minutes. Press the START button to begin cooking.
7. Once the shrimp are pink and opaque, remove them from the Air Fryer.
8. Garnish with chopped fresh parsley and serve warm.

Cajun Salmon

Serves: 4

|PREP TIME: 10 minutes
|COOK TIME: 12 minutes

4 salmon fillets
2 tbsps. olive oil
1 tbsp. Cajun seasoning
½ tsp. salt
¼ tsp. black pepper
Lemon wedges for serving

1. In a small bowl, mix the olive oil, Cajun seasoning, salt, and black pepper.
2. Rub the seasoning mixture evenly over the salmon fillets.
3. Lightly grease one wire rack.
4. Arrange the salmon fillets on the wire rack in a single layer.
5. Position the drip tray on the floor of the unit for easy cleaning.
6. Insert the wire rack into the Air Fryer. Close the door.
7. Select the AIR FRY function, choose the FISH icon, set the temperature to 375°F, and the time to 12 minutes. Press the START button to begin cooking.
8. Once the salmon is cooked through and flaky, remove it from the Air Fryer.
9. Serve warm with lemon wedges.

Fish Tacos

4 white fish fillets (such as cod or tilapia)
1 cup all-purpose flour
2 large eggs, beaten
1 cup panko bread crumbs
1 tsp. chili powder
½ tsp. garlic powder
½ tsp. salt
8 small flour tortillas
1 cup shredded cabbage
½ cup salsa
¼ cup sour cream
Lime wedges for serving

|PREP TIME: 15 minutes
|COOK TIME: 12 minutes

1. In a shallow bowl, mix the flour with chili powder, garlic powder, and salt.
2. Place the beaten eggs in another shallow bowl.
3. Place the panko bread crumbs in a third shallow bowl.
4. Dredge each fish fillet in the flour mixture, then dip in the beaten eggs, and coat with panko bread crumbs.
5. Lightly grease one wire rack.
6. Arrange the breaded fish fillets on the wire rack in a single layer.
7. Position the drip tray on the floor of the unit for easy cleaning.
8. Insert the wire rack into the Air Fryer. Close the door.
9. Select the AIR FRY function, choose the FISH icon, set the temperature to 375°F, and the time to 12 minutes. Press the START button to begin cooking.
10. Once the fish fillets are golden brown and crispy, remove them from the Air Fryer.
11. Assemble the tacos by placing a piece of fish on each tortilla, topped with shredded cabbage, salsa, and a dollop of sour cream.
12. Serve with lime wedges.

Herb-Crusted Cod with Cherry Tomatoes and Cheddar Biscuits

For the Cod:
4 cod fillets
3 tbsps. olive oil
1 cup panko bread crumbs
½ cup grated Parmesan cheese
1 tsp. dried basil
1 tsp. dried oregano
1 tsp. garlic powder
½ tsp. salt
¼ tsp. black pepper

For the Cherry Tomatoes:
1 pint cherry tomatoes
1 tbsp. olive oil
½ tsp. salt
¼ tsp. black pepper
1 tsp. dried thyme
For the Biscuits:
1½ cups all-purpose flour
1 tbsp. baking powder
1 tsp. salt
½ cup cold unsalted butter, cubed
¾ cup shredded cheddar cheese
½ cup milk

|PREP TIME: 10 minutes
|COOK TIME: 12 minutes

For the Cod:
1. In a small bowl, mix the panko bread crumbs, Parmesan cheese, dried basil, dried oregano, garlic powder, salt, and black pepper.
2. Brush the cod fillets with olive oil and press the herb mixture onto the top of each fillet.
3. Arrange the cod fillets on one greased wire rack in a single layer.
For the Cherry Tomatoes:
4. In a large bowl, toss the cherry tomatoes with olive oil, salt, black pepper, and dried thyme until evenly coated.
5. Spread the cherry tomatoes evenly on the second greased wire rack.
For the Biscuits:
6. In a large bowl, whisk together the flour, baking powder, and salt.
7. Cut in the cold butter until the mixture resembles coarse crumbs.
8. Stir in the cheddar cheese and milk until just combined.
9. Drop spoonfuls of the dough onto the third lightly greased wire rack.
10. Position the drip tray on the floor of the unit for easy cleaning.
11. Insert the wire racks with cod, cherry tomatoes, and cheddar biscuits into the Air Fryer. Close the door.
12. Select the AIR FRY function, choose the FISH icon, set the temperature to 375°F, and the time to 12 minutes. Press the START button to begin cooking.
13. Halfway through the cooking time, switch the rack positions from top to bottom to ensure even cooking.
14. Once the cod is cooked through and flaky, the cherry tomatoes are tender, and the biscuits are golden brown, remove them from the Air Fryer.
15. Serve warm.

Garlic Butter Lobster Tails

Serves: 2

|PREP TIME: 10 minutes
|COOK TIME: 10 minutes

2 lobster tails
4 tbsps. unsalted butter, melted
2 cloves garlic, minced
1 tbsp. lemon juice
½ tsp. salt
¼ tsp. black pepper
Fresh parsley for garnish

1. Use kitchen shears to cut the top of the lobster shells lengthwise down the center. Gently pull the lobster meat out and lay it on top of the shells.
2. In a small bowl, mix the melted butter, minced garlic, lemon juice, salt, and black pepper.
3. Brush the garlic butter mixture generously over the lobster meat.
4. Lightly grease one wire rack.
5. Arrange the lobster tails on the wire rack.
6. Position the drip tray on the floor of the unit for easy cleaning.
7. Insert the wire rack into the Air Fryer. Close the door.
8. Select the AIR FRY function, choose the FISH icon, set the temperature to 390°F, and the time to 10 minutes. Press the START button to begin cooking.
9. Once the lobster meat is opaque and cooked through, remove it from the Air Fryer.
10. Garnish with fresh parsley and serve warm.

Crab Cakes with Lemon Wedges

Serves: 4

|PREP TIME: 15 minutes
|COOK TIME: 12 minutes

1 lb. lump crab meat
¼ cup mayonnaise
1 large egg, beaten
1 tsp. Dijon mustard
1 tsp. Worcestershire sauce
½ tsp. Old Bay seasoning
¼ cup finely chopped green onions
½ cup panko bread crumbs
Lemon wedges for serving

1. In a large bowl, gently mix together the crab meat, mayonnaise, beaten egg, Dijon mustard, Worcestershire sauce, Old Bay seasoning, green onions, and panko bread crumbs.
2. Form the mixture into 8 patties.
3. Lightly grease one wire rack.
4. Arrange the crab cakes on the wire rack in a single layer.
5. Position the drip tray on the floor of the unit for easy cleaning.
6. Insert the wire rack into the Air Fryer. Close the door.
7. Select the AIR FRY function, choose the FISH icon, set the temperature to 400°F, and the time to 12 minutes. Press the START button to begin cooking.
8. Once the crab cakes are golden brown and crispy, remove them from the Air Fryer.
9. Serve warm with lemon wedges.

Teriyaki Salmon and Broccoli

Serves: 4

For the Salmon:
4 salmon fillets
¼ cup soy sauce
2 tbsps. honey
1 tbsp. rice vinegar
1 tbsp. sesame oil
2 cloves garlic, minced

1 tsp. grated ginger
For the Broccoli:
1 large head of broccoli, cut into florets
2 tbsps. olive oil
½ tsp. salt
¼ tsp. black pepper

|PREP TIME: 15 minutes, plus 15 minutes for marinating
|COOK TIME: 12 minutes

For the Salmon:
1. In a small bowl, whisk together the soy sauce, honey, rice vinegar, sesame oil, minced garlic, and grated ginger.
2. Place the salmon fillets in a shallow dish and pour the marinade over them. Let them marinate for 15 minutes.
3. Lightly grease one wire rack.
4. Arrange the salmon fillets on the wire rack in a single layer.
For the Broccoli:
5. In a large bowl, toss the broccoli florets with olive oil, salt, and black pepper until evenly coated.
6. Lightly grease another wire rack.
7. Spread the broccoli florets evenly on the wire rack.
8. Position the drip tray on the floor of the unit for easy cleaning.
9. Insert the wire racks with salmon and broccoli into the Air Fryer. Close the door.
10. Select the AIR FRY function, choose the FISH icon, set the temperature to 390°F, and the time to 12 minutes. Press the START button to begin cooking.
11. Halfway through the cooking time, switch the rack positions from top to bottom to ensure even cooking.
12. Once the salmon is cooked through and flaky and the broccoli is tender, remove them from the Air Fryer.
13. Serve warm.

Miso Glazed Halibut

Serves: 8

8 halibut fillets
½ cup white miso paste
4 tbsps. soy sauce
4 tbsps. mirin
2 tbsps. honey
2 tsps. sesame oil
4 green onions, sliced (for garnish)

|PREP TIME: 10 minutes
|COOK TIME: 12 minutes

1. In a small bowl, whisk together the miso paste, soy sauce, mirin, honey, and sesame oil until smooth.
2. Brush the miso glaze evenly over the halibut fillets.
3. Lightly grease two wire racks.
4. Arrange the halibut fillets on the wire racks in a single layer.
5. Position the drip tray on the floor of the unit for easy cleaning.
6. Insert the wire racks into the Air Fryer. Close the door.
7. Select the AIR FRY function, choose the FISH icon, set the temperature to 375°F, and the time to 12 minutes. Press the START button to begin cooking.
8. Halfway through the cooking time, switch the rack positions from top to bottom to ensure even cooking.
9. Once the halibut is cooked through and flaky, remove it from the Air Fryer.
10. Garnish with sliced green onions and serve warm.

Coconut Shrimp

Serves: 4

|PREP TIME: 15 minutes
|COOK TIME: 10 minutes

1 lb. large shrimp, peeled and deveined
½ cup all-purpose flour
2 large eggs, beaten
1 cup shredded coconut
½ cup panko bread crumbs
½ tsp. salt
¼ tsp. black pepper
Sweet chili sauce for serving

1. In a shallow bowl, mix the flour with salt and black pepper.
2. Place the beaten eggs in another shallow bowl.
3. In a third shallow bowl, mix the shredded coconut and panko bread crumbs.
4. Dredge each shrimp in the flour mixture, then dip in the beaten eggs, and coat with the coconut and panko mixture.
5. Lightly grease one wire rack.
6. Arrange the breaded shrimp on the wire rack in a single layer.
7. Position the drip tray on the floor of the unit for easy cleaning.
8. Insert the wire rack into the Air Fryer. Close the door.
9. Select the AIR FRY function, choose the FISH icon, set the temperature to 375°F, and the time to 10 minutes. Press the START button to begin cooking.
10. Once the shrimp are golden brown and crispy, remove them from the Air Fryer.
11. Serve warm with sweet chili sauce.

Scallops with Lemon Butter

Serves: 6

|PREP TIME: 10 minutes
|COOK TIME: 10 minutes

2 lbs. large sea scallops
4 tbsps. olive oil
1 tsp. salt
½ tsp. black pepper
8 tbsps. unsalted butter
4 cloves garlic, minced
2 lemons, juiced
Fresh parsley for garnish

1. Pat the scallops dry with paper towels and season with salt and black pepper.
2. In a small bowl, mix the olive oil, melted butter, minced garlic, and lemon juice.
3. Brush the lemon butter mixture evenly over the scallops.
4. Lightly grease two wire racks.
5. Arrange the scallops on the wire racks in a single layer.
6. Position the drip tray on the floor of the unit for easy cleaning.
7. Insert the wire racks into the Air Fryer. Close the door.
8. Select the AIR FRY function, choose the FISH icon, set the temperature to 400°F, and the time to 10 minutes. Press the START button to begin cooking.
9. Once the scallops are opaque and cooked through, remove them from the Air Fryer.
10. Garnish with fresh parsley and serve warm.

Fish and Chips

Serves: 4

For the Fish:
4 white fish fillets (such as cod or haddock)
1 cup all-purpose flour
2 large eggs, beaten
1 cup panko bread crumbs
1 tsp. paprika
½ tsp. garlic powder
½ tsp. salt

¼ tsp. black pepper
For the Chips:
2 large potatoes, cut into fries
2 tbsps. olive oil
½ tsp. salt
¼ tsp. black pepper
½ tsp. paprika

|PREP TIME: 15 minutes
|COOK TIME: 15 minutes

For the Fish:
1. In a shallow bowl, mix the flour with paprika, garlic powder, salt, and black pepper.
2. Place the beaten eggs in another shallow bowl.
3. Place the panko bread crumbs in a third shallow bowl.
4. Dredge each fish fillet in the flour mixture, then dip in the beaten eggs, and coat with panko bread crumbs.
5. Lightly grease one wire rack.
6. Arrange the breaded fish fillets on the wire rack in a single layer.
For the Chips:
7. In a large bowl, toss the potato fries with olive oil, salt, black pepper, and paprika.
8. Lightly grease another wire rack.
9. Spread the seasoned potato fries evenly on the wire rack.
10. Position the drip tray on the floor of the unit for easy cleaning.
11. Insert the wire racks with fish and chips into the Air Fryer. Close the door.
12. Select the AIR FRY function, choose the FISH icon, set the temperature to 375°F, and the time to 15 minutes. Press the START button to begin cooking.
13. Halfway through the cooking time, switch the rack positions from top to bottom to ensure even cooking.
14. Once the fish fillets are golden brown and the fries are crispy, remove them from the Air Fryer.
15. Serve warm.

Lemon Dill Salmon Jerky

Serves: 6

2 lbs. salmon fillets, skinned and sliced into ¼-inch strips
¼ cup lemon juice
2 tbsps. soy sauce
2 tbsps. maple syrup
1 tbsp. dill weed
1 tsp. garlic powder
½ tsp. sea salt

|PREP TIME: 15 minutes, plus 4 hours for marinating
|COOK TIME: 5 hours

1. In a large bowl, combine lemon juice, soy sauce, maple syrup, dill weed, garlic powder, and sea salt.
2. Add the salmon strips to the marinade, ensuring they are fully submerged. Cover and refrigerate for at least 4 hours, preferably overnight.
3. Drain the salmon strips and pat dry with paper towels.
4. Arrange the salmon strips on the wire racks, ensuring they do not overlap.
5. Position the drip tray on the floor of the unit for easy cleaning.
6. Insert the wire racks into the Air Fryer. Close the door.
7. Select the DEHYDRATE function. Choose the FISH icon, set the temperature to 165°F and the time to 5 hours.
8. Press the START button to begin dehydration.
9. Halfway through the dehydration process, open the air fryer door and switch the rack positions from top to bottom for even drying.
10. After 5 hours, check the salmon jerky for dryness. If it is not completely dry, add additional time in 30-minute increments until it reaches the desired texture.
11. Remove the salmon jerky from the air fryer and let it cool completely.
12. Store in an airtight container at room temperature for up to 2 weeks.

CHAPTER 4

Beef

BBQ Beef Ribs

3 lbs. beef short ribs
1 cup BBQ sauce
¼ cup brown sugar
2 tbsps. apple cider vinegar
1 tsp. smoked paprika
1 tsp. garlic powder
½ tsp. salt
½ tsp. black pepper

|PREP TIME: 15 minutes
|COOK TIME: 25 minutes

1. In a large bowl, mix together the BBQ sauce, brown sugar, apple cider vinegar, smoked paprika, garlic powder, salt, and black pepper.
2. Coat the beef ribs with the BBQ sauce mixture.
3. Lightly grease two wire racks.
4. Arrange the beef ribs on the wire racks in a single layer.
5. Position the drip tray on the floor of the unit for easy cleaning.
6. Insert the wire racks into the Air Fryer. Close the door.
7. Select the AIR FRY function, choose the MEAT icon, set the temperature to 375°F, and the time to 25 minutes. Press the START button to begin cooking.
8. Once the ribs are tender and caramelized, remove them from the Air Fryer.
9. Serve warm with extra BBQ sauce if desired.

Classic Beef Meatballs

1 lb. ground beef
½ cup breadcrumbs
¼ cup grated Parmesan cheese
¼ cup milk
1 large egg
2 cloves garlic, minced
1 tbsp. chopped fresh parsley
1 tsp. salt
½ tsp. black pepper
½ tsp. dried oregano

|PREP TIME: 15 minutes
|COOK TIME: 12 minutes

1. In a large bowl, combine the ground beef, breadcrumbs, Parmesan cheese, milk, egg, garlic, parsley, salt, black pepper, and oregano. Mix until well combined.
2. Form the mixture into 1-inch meatballs.
3. Lightly grease one wire rack.
4. Arrange the meatballs on the wire rack in a single layer.
5. Position the drip tray on the floor of the unit for easy cleaning.
6. Insert the wire rack into the Air Fryer. Close the door.
7. Select the AIR FRY function, choose the MEAT icon, set the temperature to 400°F, and the time to 12 minutes. Press the START button to begin cooking.
8. Once the meatballs are cooked through and golden brown, remove them from the Air Fryer.
9. Serve warm with your favorite dipping sauce.

Beef Wellington Bites

Serves: 4

|PREP TIME: 30 minutes
|COOK TIME: 14 minutes

1 lb. beef tenderloin, cut into 1-inch cubes
1 sheet puff pastry, thawed and cut into 8 squares
½ cup mushrooms, finely chopped
1 shallot, finely chopped
2 cloves garlic, minced

1 tbsp. olive oil
1 egg, beaten
1 tbsp. Dijon mustard
1 tsp. salt
½ tsp. black pepper

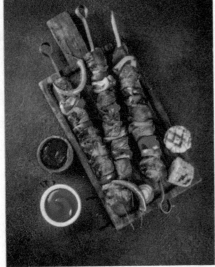

1. In a skillet, heat olive oil over medium heat and sauté the mushrooms, shallots, and garlic until softened and any liquid has evaporated. Season with salt and black pepper.
2. Pat the beef cubes dry with paper towels and season with salt and black pepper.
3. Roll out the puff pastry and cut into 8 squares. Spread a small amount of Dijon mustard in the center of each square.
4. Place a beef cube in the center of each pastry square and top with a spoonful of the mushroom mixture. Fold the corners of the pastry over the beef and pinch to seal.
5. Lightly grease one wire rack.
6. Arrange the beef Wellington bites on the wire rack.
7. Brush the pastry with the beaten egg.
8. Position the drip tray on the floor of the unit for easy cleaning.
9. Insert the wire rack into the Air Fryer. Close the door.
10. Select the BAKE function, set the temperature to 400°F, and the time to 14 minutes. Press the START button to begin cooking.
11. Once the pastry is golden brown and the beef is cooked to your desired doneness, remove the bites from the Air Fryer.
12. Serve warm.

Teriyaki Beef Skewers

Serves: 6

|PREP TIME: 15 minutes, plus 15 minutes for marinating
|COOK TIME: 12 minutes

2 lbs. beef sirloin, cut into 1-inch cubes
¼ cup soy sauce
2 tbsps. honey
1 tbsp. rice vinegar
1 tbsp. sesame oil
2 cloves garlic, minced
1 tsp. grated ginger
1 red bell pepper, cut into 1-inch pieces
1 green bell pepper, cut into 1-inch pieces
1 red onion, cut into 1-inch pieces

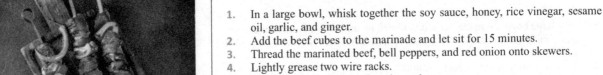

1. In a large bowl, whisk together the soy sauce, honey, rice vinegar, sesame oil, garlic, and ginger.
2. Add the beef cubes to the marinade and let sit for 15 minutes.
3. Thread the marinated beef, bell peppers, and red onion onto skewers.
4. Lightly grease two wire racks.
5. Arrange the skewers on the wire racks.
6. Position the drip tray on the floor of the unit for easy cleaning.
7. Insert the wire racks into the Air Fryer. Close the door.
8. Select the AIR FRY function, choose the MEAT icon, set the temperature to 375°F, and the time to 12 minutes. Press the START button to begin cooking.
9. Once the beef is cooked to your desired level of doneness, remove the skewers from the Air Fryer.
10. Serve warm with extra teriyaki sauce if desired.

Beef and Tender Vegetables

Serves: 6

1½ lbs. beef flank steak, thinly sliced
3 tbsps. soy sauce
1 tbsp. oyster sauce
1 tbsp. hoisin sauce
1 tbsp. sesame oil
3 cloves garlic, minced
1 tbsp. grated ginger
2 cups broccoli florets
1 red bell pepper, sliced

|PREP TIME: 15 minutes, plus 15 minutes for marinating
|COOK TIME: 10 minutes

1. In a large bowl, mix together the soy sauce, oyster sauce, hoisin sauce, sesame oil, garlic, and ginger.
2. Add the beef slices to the marinade and let sit for 15 minutes.
3. Lightly grease two wire racks.
4. Arrange the marinated beef slices on one wire rack.
5. Arrange the broccoli and bell pepper on the other wire rack.
6. Position the drip tray on the floor of the unit for easy cleaning.
7. Insert the wire racks into the Air Fryer. Close the door.
8. Select the AIR FRY function, set the temperature to 375°F, and the time to 10 minutes. Press the START button to begin cooking.
9. Once the beef is cooked through and the vegetables are tender, remove them from the Air Fryer.
10. Serve warm over rice or noodles.

Ribeye Steaks with Garlic Herb Butter

Serves: 4

4 ribeye steaks (1 inch thick)
4 tbsps. unsalted butter, softened
3 cloves garlic, minced
1 tbsp. fresh rosemary, chopped
1 tbsp. fresh thyme, chopped
1 tsp. salt
½ tsp. black pepper

|PREP TIME: 10 minutes
|COOK TIME: 10 minutes

1. In a small bowl, mix the softened butter, minced garlic, rosemary, thyme, salt, and black pepper to make the garlic herb butter.
2. Pat the ribeye steaks dry with paper towels and season both sides with salt and black pepper.
3. Lightly grease one wire rack.
4. Place the ribeye steaks on the wire rack.
5. Position the drip tray on the floor of the unit for easy cleaning.
6. Insert the wire rack into the Air Fryer. Close the door.
7. Select the AIR FRY function, choose the MEAT icon, set the temperature to 400°F, and the time to 10 minutes. Press the START button to begin cooking.
8. Once the steaks reach the desired doneness, remove them from the Air Fryer and top each steak with a dollop of garlic herb butter.
9. Let the steaks rest for 5 minutes before serving.

Crusted Beef Tenderloin with Butternut Squash and Spiced Nuts

|PREP TIME: 10 minutes
|COOK TIME: 25 minutes

For the Beef Tenderloin:
2 lbs. beef tenderloin
2 tbsps. olive oil
2 tbsps. crushed black peppercorns
1 tsp. salt
For the Butternut Squash:
1 medium butternut squash, peeled, seeded, and cut into cubes
3 tbsps. olive oil
1 tsp. ground cinnamon
½ tsp. salt
½ tsp. black pepper
For the Nuts:
2 cups mixed nuts (almonds, cashews, pecans)
2 tbsps. maple syrup
1 tsp. ground cinnamon
½ tsp. cayenne pepper
½ tsp. salt

For the Beef Tenderloin:
1. Pat the beef tenderloin dry with paper towels and brush with olive oil.
2. Press the crushed black peppercorns and salt onto the surface of the beef.
3. Place the beef tenderloin on one greased wire rack.
For the Butternut Squash:
4. In a large bowl, toss the butternut squash cubes with olive oil, ground cinnamon, salt, and black pepper until evenly coated.
5. Spread the butternut squash cubes evenly on the second greased wire rack.
For the Nuts:
6. In a large bowl, toss the mixed nuts with maple syrup, ground cinnamon, cayenne pepper, and salt until evenly coated.
7. Spread the nuts evenly on the third greased wire rack.
8. Position the drip tray on the floor of the unit for easy cleaning.
9. Insert the wire racks with beef tenderloin and butternut squash into the Air Fryer. Close the door.
10. Select the AIR FRY function, set the temperature to 375°F, and the time to 25 minutes. Press the START button to begin cooking.
11. After 15 minutes, switch the rack positions from top to bottom to ensure even cooking. Insert the wire rack with nuts into the Air Fryer. Press the START button to continue cooking.
12. With 5 minutes remaining, switch the rack positions from top to bottom again.
13. Once the beef is cooked through, the butternut squash is tender, and the spiced nuts are toasted, remove them from the Air Fryer.
14. Let the beef rest for 10 minutes before slicing. Serve warm.

Teriyaki Beef Jerky

Serves: 8

2 lbs. beef sirloin, sliced into ¼-inch strips
½ cup soy sauce
¼ cup brown sugar
2 tbsps. honey
2 tbsps. apple cider vinegar
1 tbsp. Worcestershire sauce
1 tsp. garlic powder
1 tsp. onion powder
½ tsp. black pepper

|PREP TIME: 15 minutes, plus 4 hours for marinating
|COOK TIME: 5 hours

1. In a large bowl, combine soy sauce, brown sugar, honey, apple cider vinegar, Worcestershire sauce, garlic powder, onion powder, and black pepper.
2. Add the beef strips to the marinade, ensuring they are fully submerged. Cover and refrigerate for at least 4 hours, preferably overnight.
3. Drain the beef strips and pat dry with paper towels.
4. Arrange the beef strips on the wire racks, ensuring they do not overlap.
5. Position the drip tray on the floor of the unit for easy cleaning.
6. Insert the wire racks into the Air Fryer. Close the door.
7. Select the DEHYDRATE function. Choose the MEAT icon, set the temperature to 165°F and the time to 5 hours.
8. Press the START button to begin dehydration.
9. Halfway through the dehydration process, open the air fryer door and switch the rack positions from top to bottom for even drying.
10. After 5 hours, check the beef jerky for dryness. If it is not completely dry, add additional time in 30-minute increments until it reaches the desired texture.
11. Remove the beef jerky from the air fryer and let it cool completely.
12. Store in an airtight container at room temperature for up to 2 weeks.

Beef Tenderloin with Red Wine Reduction

Serves: 6

2 lbs. beef tenderloin, trimmed and tied
2 tbsps. olive oil
1 tsp. salt
½ tsp. black pepper
1 cup red wine
½ cup beef broth
2 shallots, finely chopped
2 cloves garlic, minced
2 tbsps. unsalted butter
1 tbsp. fresh thyme, chopped

|PREP TIME: 20 minutes
|COOK TIME: 15 minutes

1. Pat the beef tenderloin dry with paper towels and season with olive oil, salt, and black pepper.
2. Lightly grease one wire rack.
3. Place the beef tenderloin on the wire rack.
4. Position the drip tray on the floor of the unit for easy cleaning.
5. Insert the wire rack into the Air Fryer. Close the door.
6. Select the AIR FRY function, choose the MEAT icon, set the temperature to 375°F, and the time to 15 minutes. Press the START button to begin cooking.
7. While the beef is cooking, prepare the red wine reduction. In a small saucepan, heat 1 tbsp. olive oil over medium heat and sauté the shallots and garlic until softened.
8. Add the red wine, beef broth, and thyme, and bring to a boil. Reduce the heat and simmer until the liquid is reduced by half. Stir in the butter.
9. Once the beef tenderloin reaches the desired doneness, remove it from the Air Fryer and let it rest for 10 minutes.
10. Slice the beef tenderloin and serve with the red wine reduction.

Garlic Butter Steak Bites

Serves: 4

|PREP TIME: 10 minutes

|COOK TIME: 10 minutes

1 lb. sirloin steak, cut into bite-sized pieces
3 tbsps. unsalted butter, melted
3 cloves garlic, minced
1 tbsp. chopped fresh parsley
1 tsp. salt
½ tsp. black pepper

1. In a large bowl, toss the steak bites with melted butter, minced garlic, parsley, salt, and black pepper until evenly coated.
2. Lightly grease one wire rack.
3. Arrange the steak bites on the wire rack in a single layer.
4. Position the drip tray on the floor of the unit for easy cleaning.
5. Insert the wire rack into the Air Fryer. Close the door.
6. Select the AIR FRY function, choose the MEAT icon, set the temperature to 400°F, and the time to 10 minutes. Press the START button to begin cooking.
7. Once the steak bites are cooked to your desired level of doneness, remove them from the Air Fryer.
8. Serve warm.

Air Fried Steak Fajitas

Serves: 6

|PREP TIME: 20 minutes, plus 15 minutes for marinating

|COOK TIME: 12 minutes

2 lbs. skirt steak
2 bell peppers (any color), sliced
1 large onion, sliced
3 tbsps. olive oil
3 cloves garlic, minced
2 tsps. ground cumin
2 tsps. chili powder

1 tsp. smoked paprika
1 tsp. salt
½ tsp. black pepper
Juice of 2 limes
12 small flour tortillas
Optional toppings: sour cream, salsa, guacamole, shredded cheese

1. In a large bowl, mix the olive oil, garlic, cumin, chili powder, smoked paprika, salt, black pepper, and lime juice.
2. Marinate the skirt steak in the mixture for 15 minutes.
3. Lightly grease one wire rack.
4. Arrange the marinated steak on one wire rack.
5. On another lightly greased wire rack, arrange the sliced bell peppers and onion.
6. Position the drip tray on the floor of the unit for easy cleaning.
7. Insert the wire racks into the Air Fryer. Close the door.
8. Select the AIR FRY function, choose the MEAT icon, set the temperature to 400°F, and the time to 12 minutes. Press the START button to begin cooking.
9. Once the steak is cooked to your desired level of doneness and the vegetables are tender, remove them from the Air Fryer.
10. Slice the steak against the grain and serve with the roasted vegetables on tortillas, along with your favorite toppings.

Marinated Flank Steak with Cauliflower and Plantain Chips

Serves: 4

For the Flank Steak:
1½ lbs. flank steak
¼ cup soy sauce
2 tbsps. olive oil
2 tbsps. Worcestershire sauce
2 cloves garlic, minced
1 tsp. dried oregano
1 tsp. ground cumin
½ tsp. salt
½ tsp. black pepper
For the Cauliflower:
1 large head of cauliflower, cut into florets
3 tbsps. olive oil
1 tsp. smoked paprika
½ tsp. salt
½ tsp. black pepper
For the Plantain Chips:
2 green plantains, peeled and thinly sliced
2 tbsps. olive oil
1 tsp. salt

|PREP TIME: 20 minutes, plus 20 minutes for marinating
|COOK TIME: 20 minutes

For the Flank Steak:
1.   In a large bowl, mix the soy sauce, olive oil, Worcestershire sauce, garlic, oregano, cumin, salt, and black pepper.
2.   Marinate the flank steak in the mixture for at least 20 minutes.
3.   Place the marinated flank steak on one greased wire rack.
For the Cauliflower:
4.   In a large bowl, toss the cauliflower florets with olive oil, smoked paprika, salt, and black pepper until evenly coated.
5.   Spread the cauliflower florets evenly on the second greased wire rack.
For the Plantain Chips:
6.   In a large bowl, toss the plantain slices with olive oil and salt until evenly coated.
7.   Spread the plantain slices evenly on the third greased wire rack.
8.   Position the drip tray on the floor of the unit for easy cleaning.
9.   Insert the wire racks with flank steak and cauliflower into the Air Fryer. Close the door.
10.   Select the AIR FRY function, set the temperature to 375°F, and the time to 20 minutes. Press the START button to begin cooking.
11.   After 10 minutes, switch the rack positions from top to bottom to ensure even cooking. Insert the rack with the plantain chips to the Air Fryer, positioning it in the middle.
12.   Continue cooking for the remaining 10 minutes, switching the rack positions once more halfway through to ensure even cooking.
13.   Once the flank steak is cooked through, the cauliflower is tender, and the plantain chips are crispy, remove them from the Air Fryer.
14.   Let flank steak rest for 5 minutes before slicing against the grain. Serve warm.

CHAPTER 5
Vegetables

Garlic Parmesan Asparagus Spears

Serves: 4

1 lb. asparagus, trimmed
2 tbsps. olive oil
¼ cup grated Parmesan cheese
1 tsp. garlic powder
½ tsp. Italian seasoning
½ tsp. salt
¼ tsp. black pepper

|PREP TIME: 5 minutes
|COOK TIME: 12 minutes

1. In a large bowl, toss the asparagus with olive oil, Parmesan cheese, garlic powder, Italian seasoning, salt, and black pepper until evenly coated.
2. Lightly grease one wire rack.
3. Spread the asparagus evenly on the wire rack.
4. Position the drip tray on the floor of the unit for easy cleaning.
5. Insert the wire rack into the Air Fryer. Close the door.
6. Select the AIR FRY function, choose the VEGETABLES icon, set the temperature to 375°F, and the time to 12 minutes. Press the START button to begin cooking.
7. Halfway through the cooking time, flip the asparagus to ensure even cooking.
8. Once the asparagus is tender and slightly crispy, remove them from the Air Fryer.
9. Serve warm.

Crispy Brussels Sprouts with Balsamic Glaze

Serves: 4

1 lb. Brussels sprouts, trimmed and halved
2 tbsps. olive oil
2 tbsps. balsamic vinegar
1 tbsp. honey
1 tsp. garlic powder
½ tsp. salt
½ tsp. black pepper

|PREP TIME: 10 minutes
|COOK TIME: 20 minutes

1. In a large bowl, toss the Brussels sprouts with olive oil, balsamic vinegar, honey, garlic powder, salt, and black pepper until evenly coated.
2. Lightly grease one wire rack.
3. Spread the Brussels sprouts evenly on the wire rack.
4. Position the drip tray on the floor of the unit for easy cleaning.
5. Insert the wire rack into the Air Fryer. Close the door.
6. Select the AIR FRY function, choose the VEGETABLES icon, set the temperature to 390°F, and the time to 20 minutes. Press the START button to begin cooking.
7. Halfway through the cooking time, toss the Brussels sprouts to ensure even cooking.
8. Once the Brussels sprouts are crispy and browned, remove them from the Air Fryer.
9. Serve warm.

Balsamic Green Beans with Toasted Almonds

Serves: 4

|PREP TIME: 5 minutes
|COOK TIME: 12 minutes

1 lb. green beans, trimmed
2 tbsps. olive oil
2 tbsps. balsamic vinegar
¼ cup sliced almonds, toasted
1 tsp. garlic powder
½ tsp. salt
¼ tsp. black pepper

1. In a large bowl, toss the green beans with olive oil, balsamic vinegar, garlic powder, salt, and black pepper until evenly coated.
2. Lightly grease one wire rack.
3. Spread the green beans evenly on the wire rack.
4. Position the drip tray on the floor of the unit for easy cleaning.
5. Insert the wire rack into the Air Fryer. Close the door.
6. Select the AIR FRY function, choose the VEGETABLES icon, set the temperature to 390°F, and the time to 12 minutes. Press the START button to begin cooking.
7. Halfway through the cooking time, flip the green beans to ensure even cooking.
8. Once the green beans are tender and slightly crispy, remove them from the Air Fryer.
9. Sprinkle toasted almonds on top before serving.
10. Serve warm.

Honey Roasted Carrots with Thyme

Serves: 4

|PREP TIME: 5 minutes
|COOK TIME: 18 minutes

1 lb. carrots, peeled and cut into sticks
2 tbsps. honey
2 tbsps. olive oil
1 tsp. dried thyme
½ tsp. salt
¼ tsp. black pepper

1. In a large bowl, toss the carrot sticks with honey, olive oil, dried thyme, salt, and black pepper until evenly coated.
2. Lightly grease one wire rack.
3. Spread the carrots evenly on the wire rack.
4. Position the drip tray on the floor of the unit for easy cleaning.
5. Insert the wire rack into the Air Fryer. Close the door.
6. Select the AIR FRY function, choose the VEGETABLES icon, set the temperature to 390°F, and the time to 18 minutes. Press the START button to begin cooking.
7. Halfway through the cooking time, flip the carrot sticks to ensure even cooking.
8. Once the carrots are tender and glazed, remove them from the Air Fryer.
9. Serve warm.

Rotisserie Herb-Roasted Cauliflower

Serves: 4

1 small cauliflower head
2 tbsps. olive oil
1 tsp. garlic powder
1 tsp. dried thyme
1 tsp. dried rosemary
½ tsp. sea salt
½ tsp. black pepper

|PREP TIME: 10 minutes
|COOK TIME: 40 minutes

1. Remove the leaves and core from the cauliflower, keeping the head intact.
2. In a small bowl, mix together olive oil, garlic powder, thyme, rosemary, sea salt, and black pepper.
3. Brush the herb mixture all over the cauliflower, ensuring it is evenly coated.
4. Secure the cauliflower on the rotisserie spit, ensuring it is balanced. Carefully slide the spit forks onto the shaft on both ends of the cauliflower. Lock the forks in place with the screws, leaving at least 1 inch of free space on both ends of the rod.
5. Ensure the drip tray is in the bottom of the unit.
6. Guide the spit into the rotisserie position by placing the left shaft into the rotisserie gear located on the left interior wall. Once in place, lift and lay the right shaft on the rotisserie holder located on the right interior wall. Be sure that the cauliflower can rotate freely in the air fryer. Close the door.
7. Select the AIR FRY function, choose the VEGETABLES icon, set the temperature to 375°F, and the time to 40 minutes. Press the ROTATE button.
8. Press the START button to begin cooking.
9. Once cooking is complete and the cauliflower is tender and golden, carefully remove it using the fetch tool.
10. Let the cauliflower cool slightly before slicing into wedges.
11. Serve warm.

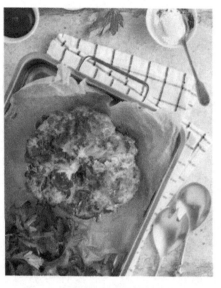

Maple Roasted Butternut Squash with Pecans

Serves: 4

1 medium butternut squash, peeled, seeded, and cut into cubes
2 tbsps. maple syrup
2 tbsps. olive oil
1 tsp. ground cinnamon
½ tsp. salt
¼ tsp. black pepper
¼ cup chopped pecans

|PREP TIME: 10 minutes
|COOK TIME: 16 minutes

1. In a large bowl, toss the butternut squash cubes with maple syrup, olive oil, ground cinnamon, salt, and black pepper until evenly coated.
2. Lightly grease one wire rack.
3. Spread the butternut squash evenly on the wire rack.
4. Position the drip tray on the floor of the unit for easy cleaning.
5. Insert the wire rack into the Air Fryer. Close the door.
6. Select the AIR FRY function, choose the VEGETABLES icon, set the temperature to 400°F, and the time to 16 minutes. Press the START button to begin cooking.
7. Halfway through the cooking time, toss the butternut squash to ensure even cooking.
8. Once the butternut squash is tender and caramelized, remove it from the Air Fryer.
9. Sprinkle chopped pecans on top before serving.

Crispy Zucchini Fries with Marinara

Serves: 4

|PREP TIME: 10 minutes
|COOK TIME: 12 minutes

2 large zucchinis, cut into fries
½ cup breadcrumbs
¼ cup grated Parmesan cheese
1 tsp. garlic powder
1 tsp. Italian seasoning
2 large eggs, beaten
1 cup marinara sauce (for serving)
½ tsp. salt
¼ tsp. black pepper

1. In a bowl, mix the breadcrumbs, Parmesan cheese, garlic powder, Italian seasoning, salt, and black pepper.
2. Dip each zucchini fry into the beaten eggs, then coat with the breadcrumb mixture.
3. Lightly grease one wire rack.
4. Arrange the zucchini fries on the wire rack in a single layer.
5. Position the drip tray on the floor of the unit for easy cleaning.
6. Insert the wire rack into the Air Fryer. Close the door.
7. Select the AIR FRY function, choose the VEGETABLES icon, set the temperature to 375°F, and the time to 12 minutes. Press the START button to begin cooking.
8. Halfway through the cooking time, flip the zucchini fries to ensure even cooking.
9. Once the zucchini fries are crispy and golden, remove them from the Air Fryer.
10. Serve warm with marinara sauce.

Lemon Garlic Broccoli and Spicy Cauliflower

Serves: 4

|PREP TIME: 5 minutes
|COOK TIME: 15 minutes

For the Broccoli:
1 large head of broccoli, cut into florets
2 tbsps. olive oil
2 cloves garlic, minced
Zest of 1 lemon
½ tsp. salt
¼ tsp. black pepper

For the Cauliflower:
1 large head of cauliflower, cut into florets
2 tbsps. olive oil
1 tsp. chili powder
1 tsp. smoked paprika
½ tsp. cumin
½ tsp. salt
¼ tsp. black pepper

For the Broccoli:
1. In a large bowl, toss the broccoli florets with olive oil, minced garlic, lemon zest, salt, and black pepper until evenly coated.
2. Lightly grease one wire rack.
3. Spread the broccoli evenly on the wire rack.
For the Cauliflower:
4. In a large bowl, toss the cauliflower florets with olive oil, chili powder, smoked paprika, cumin, salt, and black pepper until evenly coated.
5. Lightly grease another wire rack.
6. Spread the cauliflower evenly on the wire rack.
7. Position the drip tray on the floor of the unit for easy cleaning.
8. Insert the wire racks with broccoli and cauliflower into the Air Fryer. Close the door.
9. Select the AIR FRY function, choose the VEGETABLES icon, set the temperature to 375°F, and the time to 15 minutes. Press the START button to begin cooking.
10. Halfway through the cooking time, switch the rack positions from top to bottom to ensure even cooking.
11. Once the broccoli is tender and slightly crispy and the cauliflower is golden and spicy, remove them from the Air Fryer.
12. Serve warm.

Cheesy Broccoli Tots

Serves: 4

2 cups broccoli florets, finely chopped
1 cup shredded cheddar cheese
½ cup breadcrumbs
¼ cup grated Parmesan cheese
1 large egg, beaten
1 tsp. garlic powder
½ tsp. onion powder
½ tsp. salt
¼ tsp. black pepper

|PREP TIME: 15 minutes
|COOK TIME: 12 minutes

1. In a large bowl, mix the chopped broccoli, cheddar cheese, breadcrumbs, Parmesan cheese, beaten egg, garlic powder, onion powder, salt, and black pepper until well combined.
2. Shape the mixture into small tots.
3. Lightly grease one wire rack.
4. Arrange the broccoli tots on the wire rack in a single layer.
5. Position the drip tray on the floor of the unit for easy cleaning.
6. Insert the wire rack into the Air Fryer. Close the door.
7. Select the AIR FRY function, choose the VEGETABLES icon, set the temperature to 370°F, and the time to 12 minutes. Press the START button to begin cooking.
8. Halfway through the cooking time, flip the broccoli tots to ensure even cooking.
9. Once the broccoli tots are crispy and golden, remove them from the Air Fryer.
10. Serve warm.

Lemon Garlic Artichoke Hearts

Serves: 4

2 cans (14 oz. each) artichoke hearts, drained and halved
2 tbsps. olive oil
2 cloves garlic, minced
1 tsp. lemon zest
1 tbsp. lemon juice
½ tsp. dried oregano
½ tsp. salt
¼ tsp. black pepper

|PREP TIME: 10 minutes
|COOK TIME: 14 minutes

1. In a large bowl, toss the artichoke hearts with olive oil, minced garlic, lemon zest, lemon juice, dried oregano, salt, and black pepper until evenly coated.
2. Lightly grease one wire rack.
3. Spread the artichoke hearts evenly on the wire rack.
4. Position the drip tray on the floor of the unit for easy cleaning.
5. Insert the wire rack into the Air Fryer. Close the door.
6. Select the AIR FRY function, choose the VEGETABLES icon, set the temperature to 400°F, and the time to 14 minutes. Press the START button to begin cooking.
7. Halfway through the cooking time, flip the artichoke hearts to ensure even cooking.
8. Once the artichoke hearts are tender and slightly crispy, remove them from the Air Fryer.
9. Serve warm.

Crispy Okra with Ranch

Serves: 4

|PREP TIME: 10 minutes
|COOK TIME: 12 minutes

1 lb. fresh okra, cut into ½-inch pieces
½ cup cornmeal
½ cup breadcrumbs
1 tsp. paprika
1 tsp. garlic powder
½ tsp. salt
½ tsp. black pepper
2 large eggs, beaten
1 cup ranch dressing (for serving)

1. In a bowl, mix the cornmeal, breadcrumbs, paprika, garlic powder, salt, and black pepper.
2. Dip each okra piece into the beaten eggs, then coat with the cornmeal mixture.
3. Lightly grease one wire rack.
4. Arrange the okra pieces on the wire rack in a single layer.
5. Position the drip tray on the floor of the unit for easy cleaning.
6. Insert the wire rack into the Air Fryer. Close the door.
7. Select the AIR FRY function, choose the VEGETABLES icon, set the temperature to 390°F, and the time to 12 minutes. Press the START button to begin cooking.
8. Halfway through the cooking time, flip the okra pieces to ensure even cooking.
9. Once the okra is crispy and golden, remove them from the Air Fryer.
10. Serve warm with ranch dressing.

Honey Balsamic Radishes and Herb-Roasted Baby Carrots

Serves: 4

|PREP TIME: 10 minutes
|COOK TIME: 15 minutes

For the Radishes:
2 bunches radishes, trimmed and halved
2 tbsps. olive oil
1 tbsp. honey
1 tbsp. balsamic vinegar
½ tsp. salt
¼ tsp. black pepper

For the Baby Carrots:
1 lb. baby carrots
2 tbsps. olive oil
1 tsp. dried thyme
1 tsp. dried rosemary
½ tsp. garlic powder
½ tsp. salt
¼ tsp. black pepper

For the Radishes:
1. In a large bowl, toss the radishes with olive oil, honey, balsamic vinegar, salt, and black pepper until evenly coated.
2. Lightly grease one wire rack.
3. Spread the radishes evenly on the wire rack.

For the Baby Carrots:
4. In a large bowl, toss the baby carrots with olive oil, dried thyme, dried rosemary, garlic powder, salt, and black pepper until evenly coated.
5. Lightly grease another wire rack.
6. Spread the baby carrots evenly on the wire rack.
7. Position the drip tray on the floor of the unit for easy cleaning.
8. Insert the wire racks with radishes and baby carrots into the Air Fryer. Close the door.
9. Select the AIR FRY function, choose the VEGETABLES icon, set the temperature to 375°F, and the time to 15 minutes. Press the START button to begin cooking.
10. Halfway through the cooking time, switch the rack positions from top to bottom to ensure even cooking.
11. Once the radishes are tender and caramelized and the baby carrots are tender and herb-infused, remove them from the Air Fryer.
12. Serve warm.

CHAPTER 6
Poultry

Parmesan Crusted Chicken

Serves: 4

|PREP TIME: 10 minutes
|COOK TIME: 20 minutes

4 boneless, skinless chicken breasts
½ cup grated Parmesan cheese
½ cup breadcrumbs
2 tbsps. olive oil
1 tsp. garlic powder
1 tsp. Italian seasoning
½ tsp. salt
½ tsp. black pepper

1. In a large bowl, mix the Parmesan cheese, breadcrumbs, garlic powder, Italian seasoning, salt, and black pepper.
2. Brush the chicken breasts with olive oil.
3. Coat the chicken breasts with the Parmesan mixture, pressing it onto the chicken to adhere.
4. Lightly grease one wire rack.
5. Arrange the chicken breasts on the wire rack in a single layer.
6. Position the drip tray on the floor of the unit for easy cleaning.
7. Insert the wire rack into the Air Fryer. Close the door.
8. Select the AIR FRY function, choose the CHICKEN icon, set the temperature to 360°F, and the time to 20 minutes. Press the START button to begin cooking.
9. Halfway through the cooking time, flip the chicken to ensure even cooking.
10. Once the chicken is cooked through and the crust is golden brown, remove it from the Air Fryer.
11. Serve warm.

BBQ Chicken Drumsticks

Serves: 4

|PREP TIME: 10 minutes
|COOK TIME: 35 minutes

8 chicken drumsticks
½ cup BBQ sauce
2 tbsps. olive oil
1 tsp. smoked paprika
1 tsp. garlic powder
½ tsp. salt
½ tsp. black pepper

1. In a large bowl, mix the olive oil, smoked paprika, garlic powder, salt, and black pepper.
2. Add the chicken drumsticks to the bowl and toss to coat.
3. Lightly grease two wire racks.
4. Arrange 4 drumsticks on each wire rack in a single layer.
5. Position the drip tray on the floor of the unit for easy cleaning.
6. Insert the wire racks into the Air Fryer. Close the door.
7. Select the AIR FRY function, choose the CHICKEN icon, set the temperature to 375°F, and the time to 35 minutes. Press the START button to begin cooking.
8. Halfway through cooking, brush the drumsticks with BBQ sauce and flip them to ensure even cooking.
9. Once the drumsticks are cooked through and the skin is crispy, remove them from the Air Fryer.
10. Serve warm with extra BBQ sauce if desired.

Herb-Roasted Whole Chicken

1 whole chicken (3-3½ lbs.), giblets removed
2 tbsps. olive oil
1 tbsp. fresh rosemary, chopped
1 tbsp. fresh thyme, chopped
1 tbsp. fresh parsley, chopped

4 garlic cloves, minced
1 lemon, halved
1 tsp. sea salt
½ tsp. black pepper

|PREP TIME: 15 minutes
|COOK TIME: 1 hour 20 minutes

1. Rinse and pat the chicken dry. Rub the chicken with olive oil.
2. In a small bowl, mix together rosemary, thyme, parsley, garlic, sea salt, and black pepper. Rub the herb mixture all over the chicken, inside and out.
3. Insert the lemon halves inside the chicken cavity.
4. Truss the chicken tightly and secure it on the rotisserie spit, ensuring it is balanced. Run the spit through the bird lengthwise, starting at the cavity in the back. Carefully slide the spit forks onto the shaft on both ends, sinking them deep into the breast meat at one end and the thigh meat at the other end. Lock the forks in place with the screws, leaving at least 1 inch of free space on both ends of the rod.
5. Ensure the drip tray is in the bottom of the unit.
6. Guide the spit into the rotisserie position by placing the left shaft into the rotisserie gear located on the left interior wall. Once in place, lift and lay the right shaft on the rotisserie holder located on the right interior wall. Be sure that the chicken can rotate freely in the air fryer. Close the door.
7. Select the AIR FRY function, choose the CHICKEN icon, set the temperature to 375°F, and the time to 1 hour 20 minutes. Press the ROTATE button.
8. Press the START button to begin cooking.
9. Once cooking is complete and the internal temperature reaches 165°F, carefully remove the chicken using the fetch tool and let it rest for 10 minutes before carving.
10. Serve warm.

Buffalo Chicken Tenders

1½ lbs. chicken tenders
½ cup hot sauce
¼ cup melted butter
1 cup all-purpose flour
2 large eggs, beaten
1 cup breadcrumbs
½ tsp. garlic powder
½ tsp. salt
½ tsp. black pepper

|PREP TIME: 15 minutes
|COOK TIME: 12 minutes

1. In a small bowl, mix the hot sauce and melted butter.
2. In another bowl, mix the flour, garlic powder, salt, and black pepper.
3. Set up a breading station with the flour mixture, beaten eggs, and breadcrumbs in separate bowls.
4. Dip each chicken tender in the flour mixture, then the eggs, and finally coat with breadcrumbs.
5. Lightly grease one wire rack.
6. Arrange the breaded chicken tenders on the wire rack in a single layer.
7. Position the drip tray on the floor of the unit for easy cleaning.
8. Insert the wire rack into the Air Fryer. Close the door.
9. Select the AIR FRY function, choose the CHICKEN icon, set the temperature to 400°F, and the time to 12 minutes. Press the START button to begin cooking.
10. Once the chicken tenders are cooked through and crispy, remove them from the Air Fryer and toss in the hot sauce mixture.
11. Serve warm with blue cheese dressing and celery sticks.

Chipotle Lime Chicken Thighs

Serves: 4

|PREP TIME: 15 minutes
|COOK TIME: 30 minutes

8 chicken thighs
2 tbsps. olive oil
2 tbsps. chipotle in adobo sauce, chopped
2 cloves garlic, minced
Juice of 2 limes
1 tsp. smoked paprika
1 tsp. cumin
1 tsp. salt
½ tsp. black pepper

1. In a large bowl, mix the olive oil, chipotle in adobo, garlic, lime juice, smoked paprika, cumin, salt, and black pepper.
2. Add the chicken thighs to the bowl and toss to coat.
3. Lightly grease two wire racks.
4. Arrange 4 chicken thighs on each wire rack in a single layer.
5. Position the drip tray on the floor of the unit for easy cleaning.
6. Insert the wire racks into the Air Fryer. Close the door.
7. Select the AIR FRY function, choose the CHICKEN icon, set the temperature to 375°F, and the time to 30 minutes. Press the START button to begin cooking.
8. Halfway through the cooking time, switch the rack positions from top to bottom and flip the thighs to ensure even cooking.
9. Once the thighs are cooked through and crispy, remove them from the Air Fryer.
10. Serve warm with a side of lime wedges.

Mediterranean Chicken Breasts

Serves: 4

|PREP TIME: 15 minutes
|COOK TIME: 20 minutes

4 boneless, skinless chicken breasts
¼ cup olive oil
2 tbsps. lemon juice
2 cloves garlic, minced
1 tbsp. fresh oregano, chopped
1 tsp. dried thyme
1 tsp. salt
½ tsp. black pepper

1. In a small bowl, mix the olive oil, lemon juice, garlic, oregano, thyme, salt, and black pepper.
2. Brush the chicken breasts with the marinade.
3. Lightly grease one wire rack.
4. Arrange the chicken breasts on the wire rack in a single layer.
5. Position the drip tray on the floor of the unit for easy cleaning.
6. Insert the wire rack into the Air Fryer. Close the door.
7. Select the AIR FRY function, choose the CHICKEN icon, set the temperature to 360°F, and the time to 20 minutes. Press the START button to begin cooking.
8. Once the chicken breasts are cooked through and golden, remove them from the Air Fryer.
9. Serve warm.

BBQ Turkey Drumsticks with Roasted Sweet Potatoes

Serves: 4

For the Turkey Drumsticks:
4 turkey drumsticks
½ cup BBQ sauce
2 tbsps. olive oil
1 tsp. smoked paprika
½ tsp. garlic powder
½ tsp. salt
¼ tsp. black pepper
For the Sweet Potatoes:
2 tbsps. olive oil
2 large sweet potatoes, peeled and cut into cubes
1 tsp. smoked paprika
½ tsp. salt
½ tsp. black pepper

|PREP TIME: 15 minutes
|COOK TIME: 35 minutes

For the Turkey Drumsticks:
1. In a large bowl, mix the BBQ sauce, olive oil, smoked paprika, garlic powder, salt, and black pepper.
2. Add the turkey drumsticks to the mixture and toss to coat.
3. Lightly grease one wire rack.
4. Arrange the turkey drumsticks on the wire rack in a single layer.
For the Sweet Potatoes:
5. In a large bowl, toss the sweet potato cubes with olive oil, smoked paprika, salt, and black pepper until evenly coated.
6. Lightly grease another wire rack.
7. Spread the sweet potatoes evenly on the wire rack.
8. Position the drip tray on the floor of the unit for easy cleaning.
9. Insert the wire racks with turkey drumsticks and sweet potatoes into the Air Fryer. Close the door.
10. Select the AIR FRY function, choose the CHICKEN icon, set the temperature to 375°F, and the time to 35 minutes. Press the START button to begin cooking.
11. Halfway through the cooking time, switch the rack positions from top to bottom to ensure even cooking.
12. Once the turkey drumsticks are cooked through and the sweet potatoes are tender, remove them from the Air Fryer.
13. Serve warm.

Duck Breast with Roasted Brussels Sprouts

Serves: 2

|PREP TIME: 15 minutes
|COOK TIME: 20 minutes

For the Duck Breast:
2 duck breasts, skin-on
2 tbsps. olive oil
1 tsp. salt
½ tsp. black pepper
1 tsp. dried thyme

For the Brussels Sprouts:
1 lb. Brussels sprouts, trimmed and halved
2 tbsps. olive oil
1 tsp. garlic powder
½ tsp. salt
½ tsp. black pepper

For the Duck Breast:
1. Score the skin of the duck breasts in a crisscross pattern.
2. In a small bowl, mix the olive oil, salt, black pepper, and thyme.
3. Rub the mixture all over the duck breasts.
4. Lightly grease one wire rack.
5. Arrange the duck breasts on the wire rack, skin side up.
For the Brussels Sprouts:
6. In a large bowl, toss the Brussels sprouts with olive oil, garlic powder, salt, and black pepper until evenly coated.
7. Lightly grease another wire rack.
8. Spread the Brussels sprouts evenly on the wire rack.
9. Position the drip tray on the floor of the unit for easy cleaning.
10. Insert the wire racks with duck breasts and Brussels sprouts into the Air Fryer. Close the door.
11. Select the AIR FRY function, set the temperature to 375°F, and the time to 20 minutes. Press the START button to begin cooking.
12. Halfway through the cooking time, switch the rack positions from top to bottom to ensure even cooking.
13. Once the duck breasts are cooked to your desired doneness and the Brussels sprouts are tender, remove them from the Air Fryer.
14. Serve warm.

Greek Chicken Skewers

Serves: 6

|PREP TIME: 15 minutes, plus 15 minutes
for marinating
|COOK TIME: 12 minutes

2 lbs. boneless, skinless chicken thighs, cut into 1-inch pieces
¼ cup olive oil
Juice of 1 lemon
3 cloves garlic, minced
1 tbsp. dried oregano
1 tsp. dried thyme
1 tsp. salt
½ tsp. black pepper
1 red onion, cut into 1-inch pieces
2 zucchinis, sliced into rounds
1 cup cherry tomatoes

1. In a large bowl, mix the olive oil, lemon juice, garlic, oregano, thyme, salt, and black pepper.
2. Add the chicken pieces to the marinade and let sit for 15 minutes.
3. Thread the marinated chicken, onion, zucchini, and cherry tomatoes onto skewers.
4. Lightly grease two wire racks.
5. Arrange the chicken skewers on the wire racks.
6. Position the drip tray on the floor of the unit for easy cleaning.
7. Insert the wire racks into the Air Fryer. Close the door.
8. Select the AIR FRY function, set the temperature to 400°F, and the time to 12 minutes. Press the START button to begin cooking.
9. Halfway through the cooking time, flip the skewers to ensure even cooking.
10. Once the chicken is cooked through and slightly charred, remove the skewers from the Air Fryer.
11. Serve warm with a side of tzatziki sauce.

Savory Turkey Jerky

Serves: 8

2 lbs. turkey breast, sliced into ¼-inch strips
½ cup soy sauce
¼ cup Worcestershire sauce
2 tbsps. honey
1 tbsp. apple cider vinegar
1 tsp. onion powder
1 tsp. black pepper

|PREP TIME: 15 minutes, plus 4 hours for marinating
|COOK TIME: 6 hours

1. In a large bowl, combine soy sauce, Worcestershire sauce, honey, apple cider vinegar, onion powder, and black pepper.
2. Add the turkey strips to the marinade, ensuring they are fully submerged. Cover and refrigerate for at least 4 hours, preferably overnight.
3. Drain the turkey strips and pat dry with paper towels.
4. Arrange the turkey strips on the wire racks, ensuring they do not overlap.
5. Position the drip tray on the floor of the unit for easy cleaning.
6. Insert the wire racks into the Air Fryer. Close the door.
7. Select the DEHYDRATE function. choose the CHICKEN icon, set the temperature to 165°F and the time to 6 hours.
8. Press the START button to begin dehydration.
9. Halfway through the dehydration process, open the air fryer door and switch the rack positions from top to bottom for even drying.
10. After 6 hours, check the turkey jerky for dryness. If it is not completely dry, add additional time in 30-minute increments until it reaches the desired texture.
11. Remove the turkey jerky from the air fryer and let it cool completely.
12. Store in an airtight container at room temperature for up to 2 weeks.

Maple Glazed Turkey Breast

Serves: 6

2 lbs. boneless turkey breast
¼ cup maple syrup
2 tbsps. Dijon mustard
2 tbsps. olive oil
1 tsp. garlic powder
1 tsp. dried thyme
½ tsp. salt
½ tsp. black pepper

|PREP TIME: 10 minutes
|COOK TIME: 35 minutes

1. In a small bowl, mix the maple syrup, Dijon mustard, olive oil, garlic powder, thyme, salt, and black pepper.
2. Brush the turkey breast with the maple glaze.
3. Lightly grease one wire rack.
4. Place the turkey breast on the wire rack.
5. Position the drip tray on the floor of the unit for easy cleaning.
6. Insert the wire rack into the Air Fryer. Close the door.
7. Select the AIR FRY function, choose the CHICKEN icon, set the temperature to 365°F, and the time to 35 minutes. Press the START button to begin cooking.
8. Once the turkey breast is cooked through and the glaze is caramelized, remove it from the Air Fryer.
9. Let rest for 10 minutes before slicing and serving.

Spicy Chicken Wings with Green Beans and Garlic Knots

Serves: 4

|PREP TIME: 10 minutes
|COOK TIME: 30 minutes

For the Chicken Wings:
2 lbs. chicken wings
¼ cup hot sauce
2 tbsps. olive oil
1 tsp. garlic powder
1 tsp. smoked paprika
½ tsp. salt
½ tsp. black pepper
For the Green Beans
1 lb. green beans, trimmed
2 tbsps. olive oil
½ tsp. salt
¼ tsp. black pepper
½ tsp. garlic powder
For the Garlic Knots:
1 package refrigerated pizza dough
4 tbsps. unsalted butter, melted
2 cloves garlic, minced
¼ cup grated Parmesan cheese
1 tbsp. chopped fresh parsley

For the Chicken Wings:
1. In a large bowl, mix the hot sauce, olive oil, garlic powder, smoked paprika, salt, and black pepper.
2. Add the chicken wings to the bowl and toss to coat.
3. Lightly grease one wire rack.
4. Arrange the chicken wings on the wire rack in a single layer.
For the Green Beans:
5. In a large bowl, toss the green beans with olive oil, salt, black pepper, and garlic powder until evenly coated.
6. Lightly grease one wire rack.
7. Spread the green beans evenly on the wire rack.
For the Garlic Knots:
8. Roll out the pizza dough and cut into strips.
9. Tie each strip into a knot and place on a lightly greased wire rack.
10. In a small bowl, mix the melted butter and minced garlic.
11. Brush the garlic butter over the knots.
12. Sprinkle with grated Parmesan cheese and chopped parsley.
13. Position the drip tray on the floor of the unit for easy cleaning.
14. Insert the wire rack with chicken wings into the Air Fryer. Close the door.
15. Select the AIR FRY function, choose the CHICKEN icon, set the temperature to 375°F, and the time to 30 minutes. Press the START button to begin cooking.
16. After 15 minutes, insert the wire rack with green beans into the Air Fryer. Close the door and press START to continue cooking.
17. With 10 minutes remaining, insert the wire rack with knots into the Air Fryer, switching the rack positions from top to bottom to ensure even cooking. Close the door and press START to continue cooking.
18. Once the wings are cooked through, the green beans are tender, and the garlic knots are golden brown, remove them from the Air Fryer.
19. Serve warm.

CHAPTER 7
Pork

Honey Garlic Pork Chops

Serves: 8

|PREP TIME: 10 minutes
|COOK TIME: 15 minutes

8 boneless pork chops
¼ cup honey
2 tbsps. soy sauce
2 cloves garlic, minced
1 tbsp. olive oil
1 tsp. dried thyme
½ tsp. salt
½ tsp. black pepper

1. In a small bowl, mix the honey, soy sauce, garlic, olive oil, thyme, salt, and black pepper.
2. Brush the mixture over the pork chops, coating them evenly.
3. Lightly grease two wire racks.
4. Arrange 4 pork chops on each wire rack in a single layer.
5. Position the drip tray on the floor of the unit for easy cleaning.
6. Insert the wire racks into the Air Fryer. Close the door.
7. Select the AIR FRY function, choose the MEAT icon, set the temperature to 375°F, and the time to 15 minutes. Press the START button to begin cooking.
8. Halfway through the cooking time, switch the rack positions from top to bottom and flip the chops to ensure even cooking.
9. Once the pork chops are cooked through and glazed, remove them from the Air Fryer.
10. Serve warm.

Rotisserie BBQ Pork Tenderloin

Serves: 4

|PREP TIME: 10 minutes, plus 4 hours for marinating
|COOK TIME: 1 hour 10 minutes

1 pork tenderloin (2 lbs.)
½ cup BBQ sauce
2 tbsps. apple cider vinegar
1 tbsp. olive oil

1 tsp. smoked paprika
1 tsp. garlic powder
½ tsp. black pepper

1. In a large bowl, combine BBQ sauce, apple cider vinegar, olive oil, smoked paprika, garlic powder, and black pepper.
2. Add the pork tenderloin to the marinade, ensuring it is fully coated. Cover and refrigerate for at least 4 hours, preferably overnight.
3. Remove the pork tenderloin from the marinade and pat dry with paper towels.
4. Carefully push the spit lengthwise through the center of the tenderloin. Carefully slide the spit forks onto the shaft on both ends, inserting the prongs deeply into the meat. Lock the forks in place with the screws, leaving at least 1 inch of free space on both ends of the rod.
5. Ensure the drip tray is in the bottom of the unit.
6. Guide the spit into the rotisserie position by placing the left shaft into the rotisserie gear located on the left interior wall. Once in place, lift and lay the right shaft on the rotisserie holder located on the right interior wall. Be sure that the pork can rotate freely in the air fryer. Close the door.
7. Select the AIR FRY function, choose the MEAT icon, set the temperature to 375°F, and the time to 1 hour 10 minutes. Press the ROTATE button.
8. Press the START button to begin cooking.
9. Once cooking is complete and the internal temperature reaches 145°F, carefully remove the pork using the fetch tool and let it rest for 10 minutes before slicing.
10. Serve warm with extra BBQ sauce on the side.

Sweet and Spicy Pork Ribs

Serves: 4

2 lbs. pork ribs
¼ cup soy sauce
¼ cup honey
2 tbsps. apple cider vinegar
2 cloves garlic, minced
1 tbsp. sriracha sauce
1 tsp. smoked paprika
1 tsp. ground cumin
½ tsp. salt
½ tsp. black pepper

|PREP TIME: 20 minutes
|COOK TIME: 40 minutes

1. In a small bowl, mix the soy sauce, honey, apple cider vinegar, garlic, sriracha sauce, smoked paprika, cumin, salt, and black pepper.
2. Brush the mixture over the pork ribs, coating them evenly.
3. Lightly grease one wire rack.
4. Arrange the pork ribs on the wire rack in a single layer.
5. Position the drip tray on the floor of the unit for easy cleaning.
6. Insert the wire rack into the Air Fryer. Close the door.
7. Select the AIR FRY function, choose the MEAT icon, set the temperature to 350°F, and the time to 40 minutes. Press the START button to begin cooking.
8. Halfway through cooking, flip the ribs to ensure even cooking.
9. Once the pork ribs are cooked through and glazed, remove them from the Air Fryer.
10. Serve warm.

Garlic Parmesan Pork Chops with Carrot Fries

Serves: 4

For the Pork Chops:
4 boneless pork chops
2 tbsps. olive oil
½ cup grated Parmesan cheese
2 cloves garlic, minced
1 tsp. Italian seasoning
½ tsp. salt

½ tsp. black pepper
For the Carrot Fries:
1 lb. carrots, peeled and cut into fries
2 tbsps. olive oil
1 tsp. garlic powder
½ tsp. salt
½ tsp. black pepper

|PREP TIME: 10 minutes
|COOK TIME: 18 minutes

For the Pork Chops:
1. In a small bowl, mix the olive oil, Parmesan cheese, garlic, Italian seasoning, salt, and black pepper.
2. Rub the mixture all over the pork chops.
3. Lightly grease one wire rack.
4. Arrange the pork chops on the wire rack in a single layer.

For the Carrot Fries:
5. In a large bowl, toss the carrot fries with olive oil, garlic powder, salt, and black pepper until evenly coated.
6. Lightly grease another wire rack.
7. Spread the carrot fries evenly on the wire rack.
8. Position the drip tray on the floor of the unit for easy cleaning.
9. Insert the wire racks with pork chops and carrot fries into the Air Fryer. Close the door.
10. Select the AIR FRY function, set the temperature to 370°F, and the time to 18 minutes. Press the START button to begin cooking.
11. Halfway through the cooking time, switch the rack positions from top to bottom to ensure even cooking.
12. Once the pork chops are cooked through and the carrot fries are crispy, remove them from the Air Fryer.
13. Serve warm.

BBQ Pulled Pork

|PREP TIME: 10 minutes

|COOK TIME: 1 hour

2 lbs. pork shoulder
1 cup BBQ sauce
2 tbsps. brown sugar
2 tbsps. apple cider vinegar
1 tbsp. paprika
1 tsp. garlic powder
1 tsp. onion powder
1 tsp. salt
½ tsp. black pepper

1. In a small bowl, mix the BBQ sauce, brown sugar, apple cider vinegar, paprika, garlic powder, onion powder, salt, and black pepper.
2. Rub the mixture all over the pork shoulder.
3. Lightly grease one wire rack.
4. Place the pork shoulder on the wire rack.
5. Position the drip tray on the floor of the unit for easy cleaning.
6. Insert the wire rack into the Air Fryer. Close the door.
7. Select the BAKE function, set the temperature to 325°F, and the time to 1 hour. Press the START button to begin cooking.
8. Once the pork is tender and can be pulled apart with a fork, remove it from the Air Fryer.
9. Shred the pork and mix with additional BBQ sauce if desired. Serve warm.

Teriyaki Pork Skewers

|PREP TIME: 20 minutes, plus 15 minutes for marinating

|COOK TIME: 15 minutes

2 lbs. pork tenderloin, cut into 1-inch pieces
¼ cup soy sauce
2 tbsps. honey
1 tbsp. rice vinegar
1 tbsp. sesame oil
2 cloves garlic, minced
1 tsp. grated ginger

1. In a large bowl, whisk together the soy sauce, honey, rice vinegar, sesame oil, garlic, and ginger.
2. Add the pork pieces to the marinade and let sit for 15 minutes.
3. Thread the marinated pork pieces onto skewers.
4. Lightly grease two wire racks.
5. Arrange the pork skewers on the wire racks in a single layer.
6. Position the drip tray on the floor of the unit for easy cleaning.
7. Insert the wire racks into the Air Fryer. Close the door.
8. Select the AIR FRY function, choose the MEAT icon, set the temperature to 360°F, and the time to 15 minutes. Press the START button to begin cooking.
9. Halfway through the cooking time, switch the rack positions from top to bottom and flip the skewers to ensure even cooking.
10. Once the pork skewers are cooked through and slightly charred, remove them from the Air Fryer.
11. Serve warm.

Cajun Spiced Pork Chops

Serves: 6

6 boneless pork chops
2 tbsps. olive oil
1 tbsp. Cajun seasoning
1 tsp. smoked paprika
½ tsp. garlic powder
½ tsp. onion powder
½ tsp. salt
¼ tsp. black pepper

|PREP TIME: 10 minutes
|COOK TIME: 15 minutes

1. In a small bowl, mix the olive oil, Cajun seasoning, smoked paprika, garlic powder, onion powder, salt, and black pepper.
2. Brush the mixture over the pork chops, coating them evenly.
3. Lightly grease two wire racks.
4. Arrange the pork chops on the wire racks in a single layer.
5. Position the drip tray on the floor of the unit for easy cleaning.
6. Insert the wire racks into the Air Fryer. Close the door.
7. Select the AIR FRY function, choose the MEAT icon, set the temperature to 370°F, and the time to 15 minutes. Press the START button to begin cooking.
8. Halfway through the cooking time, switch the rack positions from top to bottom and flip the chops to ensure even cooking.
9. Once the pork chops are cooked through and spiced, remove them from the Air Fryer.
10. Serve warm.

Garlic Rosemary Pork Roast

Serves: 6

2½ lbs. pork roast
2 tbsps. olive oil
4 cloves garlic, minced
2 tbsps. fresh rosemary, chopped
1 tbsp. fresh thyme, chopped
1 tsp. salt
½ tsp. black pepper

|PREP TIME: 15 minutes
|COOK TIME: 45 minutes

1. In a small bowl, mix the olive oil, garlic, rosemary, thyme, salt, and black pepper.
2. Rub the mixture all over the pork roast.
3. Lightly grease one wire rack.
4. Place the pork roast on the wire rack.
5. Position the drip tray on the floor of the unit for easy cleaning.
6. Insert the wire rack into the Air Fryer. Close the door.
7. Select the AIR FRY function, choose the MEAT icon, set the temperature to 350°F, and the time to 45 minutes. Press the START button to begin cooking.
8. Once the pork roast is cooked through and fragrant, remove it from the Air Fryer.
9. Let rest for 10 minutes before slicing and serving.

BBQ Pork Ribs with Corn on the Cob

Serves: 4

|PREP TIME: 15 minutes
|COOK TIME: 40 minutes

For the Pork Ribs:
2 lbs. pork ribs
½ cup BBQ sauce
2 tbsps. brown sugar
1 tbsp. apple cider vinegar
1 tsp. smoked paprika
½ tsp. garlic powder
½ tsp. salt
½ tsp. black pepper
For the Corn on the Cob:
4 ears of corn, husked
2 tbsps. melted butter
½ tsp. salt
¼ tsp. black pepper

For the Pork Ribs:
1. In a small bowl, mix the BBQ sauce, brown sugar, apple cider vinegar, smoked paprika, garlic powder, salt, and black pepper.
2. Brush the mixture over the pork ribs, coating them evenly.
3. Lightly grease one wire rack.
4. Arrange the pork ribs on the wire rack in a single layer.
For the Corn on the Cob:
5. Brush the corn with melted butter and season with salt and black pepper.
6. Lightly grease another wire rack.
7. Arrange the corn on the cob on the wire rack.
8. Position the drip tray on the floor of the unit for easy cleaning.
9. Insert the wire rack with pork ribs into the Air Fryer. Close the door.
10. Select the AIR FRY function, set the temperature to 360°F, and the time to 40 minutes. Press the START button to begin cooking.
11. With 15 minutes remaining, insert the wire rack with corn on the cob, switching the rack positions from top to bottom to ensure even cooking. Close the door and press START to continue cooking.
12. Once the pork ribs are cooked through and the corn is tender, remove them from the Air Fryer.
13. Serve warm.

Parmesan Crusted Pork Cutlets

Serves: 4

4 boneless pork cutlets
1 cup breadcrumbs
½ cup grated Parmesan cheese
1 tsp. garlic powder
1 tsp. Italian seasoning
2 large eggs, beaten
¼ cup all-purpose flour
2 tbsps. olive oil
½ tsp. salt
½ tsp. black pepper

|PREP TIME: 15 minutes
|COOK TIME: 12 minutes

1. In a shallow dish, mix the breadcrumbs, Parmesan cheese, garlic powder, and Italian seasoning.
2. Dredge each pork cutlet in flour, then dip in beaten eggs, and finally coat with the breadcrumb mixture.
3. Lightly grease one wire rack.
4. Arrange the pork cutlets on the wire rack in a single layer.
5. Position the drip tray on the floor of the unit for easy cleaning.
6. Insert the wire rack into the Air Fryer. Close the door.
7. Select the AIR FRY function, choose the MEAT icon, set the temperature to 370°F, and the time to 12 minutes. Press the START button to begin cooking.
8. Halfway through cooking, flip the pork cutlets to ensure even cooking.
9. Once the pork cutlets are cooked through and golden brown, remove them from the Air Fryer.
10. Serve warm.

Asian Glazed Pork Belly

Serves: 6

2 lbs. pork belly, cut into 1-inch cubes
¼ cup soy sauce
2 tbsps. hoisin sauce
2 tbsps. honey
1 tbsp. rice vinegar
2 cloves garlic, minced
1 tsp. grated ginger
1 tsp. five-spice powder
½ tsp. black pepper

|PREP TIME: 20 minutes
|COOK TIME: 35 minutes

1. In a large bowl, whisk together the soy sauce, hoisin sauce, honey, rice vinegar, garlic, ginger, five-spice powder, and black pepper.
2. Add the pork belly cubes to the marinade and let sit for 15 minutes.
3. Lightly grease one wire rack.
4. Arrange the pork belly cubes on the wire rack in a single layer.
5. Position the drip tray on the floor of the unit for easy cleaning.
6. Insert the wire rack into the Air Fryer. Close the door.
7. Select the AIR FRY function, choose the MEAT icon, set the temperature to 350°F, and the time to 35 minutes. Press the START button to begin cooking.
8. Once the pork belly is cooked through and glazed, remove it from the Air Fryer.
9. Serve warm.

Hearty Pork Steaks with Potatoes and Spring Rolls

Serves: 4

|PREP TIME: 10 minutes
|COOK TIME: 20 minutes

For the Pork Steaks:
4 pork steaks
2 tbsps. olive oil
2 cloves garlic, minced
1 tsp. dried rosemary
1 tsp. dried thyme
½ tsp. salt
½ tsp. black pepper
For the Potatoes:
8 fingerling potatoes, halved
2 tbsps. olive oil
1 tsp. garlic powder
1 tsp. dried parsley
½ tsp. salt
½ tsp. black pepper
For the Spring Rolls:
8 spring roll wrappers
1 cup shredded cabbage
⅓ cup shredded carrots
⅓ cup bean sprouts
¼ cup sliced green onions
2 tbsps. soy sauce
1 tbsp. hoisin sauce
1 tsp. sesame oil
1 tbsp. vegetable oil (for brushing)

For the Pork Steaks:
1. In a small bowl, mix the olive oil, garlic, rosemary, thyme, salt, and black pepper.
2. Rub the mixture all over the pork steaks.
3. Arrange the pork steaks on one greased wire rack in a single layer.
For the Potatoes:
4. In a large bowl, toss the red potato halves with olive oil, garlic powder, dried parsley, salt, and black pepper until evenly coated.
5. Arrange the red potato halves evenly on the second greased wire rack, cut side up.
For the Spring Rolls:
6. In a large bowl, mix the shredded cabbage, shredded carrots, bean sprouts, green onions, soy sauce, hoisin sauce, and sesame oil.
7. Place a small amount of the vegetable mixture in the center of each spring roll wrapper and roll tightly.
8. Arrange the spring rolls on the third greased wire rack and brush with vegetable oil.
9. Position the drip tray on the floor of the unit for easy cleaning.
10. Insert the wire racks with pork steaks and potato halves into the Air Fryer. Close the door.
11. Select the AIR FRY function, set the temperature to 360°F, and the time to 20 minutes. Press the START button to begin cooking.
12. After 10 minutes, insert the wire rack with spring rolls into the Air Fryer, switching the rack positions from top to bottom to ensure even cooking. Close the door and press START to continue cooking.
13. Once the pork steaks are cooked through, the red potatoes are tender, and the spring rolls are crispy and golden brown, remove them from the Air Fryer.
14. Serve warm.

CHAPTER 8
Lamb

Garlic Rosemary Lamb Cutlets

|PREP TIME: 10 minutes
|COOK TIME: 12 minutes

8 lamb cutlets
2 tbsps. olive oil
2 cloves garlic, minced
1 tbsp. fresh rosemary, chopped
½ tsp. salt
½ tsp. black pepper

1. In a small bowl, mix the olive oil, minced garlic, rosemary, salt, and black pepper.
2. Rub the mixture all over the lamb cutlets.
3. Lightly grease one wire rack.
4. Arrange the lamb cutlets on the wire rack in a single layer.
5. Position the drip tray on the floor of the unit for easy cleaning.
6. Insert the wire rack into the Air Fryer. Close the door.
7. Select the AIR FRY function, choose the MEAT icon, set the temperature to 375°F, and the time to 12 minutes. Press the START button to begin cooking.
8. Halfway through the cooking time, switch the rack positions from top to bottom and flip the cutlets to ensure even cooking.
9. Once the lamb cutlets are cooked to your desired doneness, remove them from the Air Fryer.
10. Serve warm.

Honey Mustard Glazed Lamb Ribs

|PREP TIME: 15 minutes
|COOK TIME: 25 minutes

2 lbs. lamb ribs
¼ cup honey
2 tbsps. Dijon mustard
1 tbsp. soy sauce
2 cloves garlic, minced
1 tsp. smoked paprika
½ tsp. salt
½ tsp. black pepper

1. In a small bowl, mix the honey, Dijon mustard, soy sauce, minced garlic, smoked paprika, salt, and black pepper.
2. Rub the mixture all over the lamb ribs.
3. Lightly grease one wire rack.
4. Arrange the lamb ribs on the wire rack in a single layer.
5. Position the drip tray on the floor of the unit for easy cleaning.
6. Insert the wire rack into the Air Fryer. Close the door.
7. Select the AIR FRY function, choose the MEAT icon, set the temperature to 375°F, and the time to 25 minutes. Press the START button to begin cooking.
8. Halfway through the cooking time, flip the lamb ribs to ensure even cooking.
9. Once the lamb ribs are cooked to your desired doneness and caramelized, remove them from the Air Fryer.
10. Serve warm.

Lamb Kofta with Tzatziki

Serves: 4

1 lb. ground lamb
1 small onion, finely chopped
2 cloves garlic, minced
¼ cup chopped fresh parsley
1 tsp. ground cumin
1 tsp. ground coriander
½ tsp. ground cinnamon
½ tsp. salt
¼ tsp. black pepper
1 cup tzatziki sauce (for serving)

|PREP TIME: 20 minutes
|COOK TIME: 12 minutes

1. In a large bowl, mix the ground lamb, chopped onion, minced garlic, parsley, cumin, coriander, cinnamon, salt, and black pepper until well combined.
2. Shape the mixture into small sausage-like logs around wooden skewers.
3. Lightly grease one wire rack.
4. Arrange the lamb kofta on the wire rack.
5. Position the drip tray on the floor of the unit for easy cleaning.
6. Insert the wire rack into the Air Fryer. Close the door.
7. Select the AIR FRY function, choose the MEAT icon, set the temperature to 375°F, and the time to 12 minutes. Press the START button to begin cooking.
8. Halfway through the cooking time, flip the kofta to ensure even cooking.
9. Once the kofta are cooked through and slightly charred, remove them from the Air Fryer.
10. Serve warm with tzatziki sauce.

Mint Pesto Lamb Loin Chops

Serves: 8

8 lamb loin chops
2 tbsps. olive oil
2 cloves garlic, minced
¼ cup mint pesto
½ tsp. salt
½ tsp. black pepper

|PREP TIME: 10 minutes
|COOK TIME: 15 minutes

1. In a small bowl, mix the olive oil, minced garlic, mint pesto, salt, and black pepper.
2. Rub the mixture all over the lamb loin chops.
3. Lightly grease one wire rack.
4. Arrange the lamb loin chops on the wire rack in a single layer.
5. Position the drip tray on the floor of the unit for easy cleaning.
6. Insert the wire rack into the Air Fryer. Close the door.
7. Select the AIR FRY function, choose the MEAT icon, set the temperature to 375°F, and the time to 15 minutes. Press the START button to begin cooking.
8. Halfway through the cooking time, flip the lamb loin chops to ensure even cooking.
9. Halfway through the cooking time, switch the rack positions from top to bottom and flip the chops to ensure even cooking.
10. Once the lamb loin chops are cooked to your desired doneness, remove them from the Air Fryer.
11. Serve warm.

Tasty Lamb Cutlets with Mint Yogurt Sauce

Serves: 8

|PREP TIME: 15 minutes
|COOK TIME: 12 minutes

8 lamb cutlets
3 tbsps. olive oil
2 cloves garlic, minced
1 tbsp. fresh mint, chopped
1 tbsp. fresh parsley, chopped
1 tbsp. lemon juice
1 tsp. lemon zest

½ tsp. salt
¼ tsp. black pepper
1 cup plain Greek yogurt
1 tbsp. fresh mint, finely chopped (for sauce)
1 tbsp. lemon juice (for sauce)
Salt and pepper to taste (for sauce)

1. In a small bowl, mix 3 tbsps. olive oil, minced garlic, chopped mint, parsley, lemon juice, lemon zest, salt, and black pepper.
2. Rub the mixture all over the lamb cutlets.
3. Lightly grease one wire rack.
4. Arrange the lamb cutlets on the wire rack in a single layer.
5. Position the drip tray on the floor of the unit for easy cleaning.
6. Insert the wire rack into the Air Fryer. Close the door.
7. Select the AIR FRY function, choose the MEAT icon, set the temperature to 375°F, and the time to 12 minutes. Press the START button to begin cooking.
8. Halfway through the cooking time, switch the rack positions from top to bottom and flip the lamb cutlets to ensure even cooking.
9. While the lamb is cooking, prepare the mint yogurt sauce by mixing the Greek yogurt, chopped mint, lemon juice, salt, and pepper in a small bowl.
10. Once the lamb cutlets are cooked to your desired doneness, remove them from the Air Fryer.
11. Serve warm with mint yogurt sauce on the side.

Spiced Lamb Meatballs

Serves: 4

|PREP TIME: 15 minutes
|COOK TIME: 12 minutes

1 lb. ground lamb
¼ cup breadcrumbs
¼ cup grated Parmesan cheese
1 egg, beaten
2 cloves garlic, minced
1 tsp. ground cumin
1 tsp. smoked paprika
½ tsp. ground coriander
½ tsp. salt
½ tsp. black pepper

1. In a large bowl, mix the ground lamb, breadcrumbs, Parmesan cheese, beaten egg, minced garlic, cumin, smoked paprika, coriander, salt, and black pepper until well combined.
2. Shape the mixture into small meatballs.
3. Lightly grease one wire rack.
4. Arrange the meatballs on the wire rack in a single layer.
5. Position the drip tray on the floor of the unit for easy cleaning.
6. Insert the wire rack into the Air Fryer. Close the door.
7. Select the AIR FRY function, choose the MEAT icon, set the temperature to 375°F, and the time to 12 minutes. Press the START button to begin cooking.
8. Halfway through the cooking time, toss the meatballs to ensure even cooking.
9. Once the meatballs are cooked through and golden brown, remove them from the Air Fryer.
10. Serve warm.

Spicy Harissa Lamb Chops

Serves: 8

8 lamb chops
2 tbsps. olive oil
2 tbsps. harissa paste
2 cloves garlic, minced
1 tsp. ground cumin
½ tsp. salt
½ tsp. black pepper

|PREP TIME: 10 minutes
|COOK TIME: 15 minutes

1. In a small bowl, mix the olive oil, harissa paste, minced garlic, ground cumin, salt, and black pepper.
2. Rub the mixture all over the lamb chops.
3. Lightly grease one wire rack.
4. Arrange the lamb chops on the wire rack in a single layer.
5. Position the drip tray on the floor of the unit for easy cleaning.
6. Insert the wire rack into the Air Fryer. Close the door.
7. Select the AIR FRY function, choose the MEAT icon, set the temperature to 375°F, and the time to 15 minutes. Press the START button to begin cooking.
8. Halfway through the cooking time, switch the rack positions from top to bottom and flip the chops to ensure even cooking.
9. Once the lamb chops are cooked to your desired doneness, remove them from the Air Fryer.
10. Serve warm.

Rosemary-Lemon Lamb Leg

Serves: 6

1 boneless leg of lamb (3-4 lbs.)
¼ cup olive oil
4 garlic cloves, minced
2 tbsps. fresh rosemary, chopped
1 lemon, juiced
1 tsp. sea salt
½ tsp. black pepper

|PREP TIME: 15 minutes, plus 30 minutes for marinating
|COOK TIME: 1 hour 30 minutes

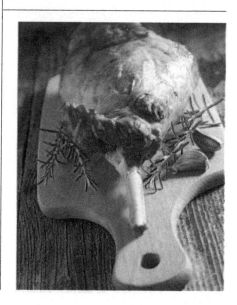

1. In a large bowl, combine olive oil, garlic, rosemary, lemon juice, sea salt, and black pepper.
2. Add the lamb to the marinade, ensuring it is fully coated. Cover and refrigerate for at least 30 minutes.
3. Remove the lamb from the marinade and pat dry with paper towels.
4. Carefully push the spit lengthwise through the center of the lamb. Carefully slide the spit forks onto the shaft on both ends, inserting the prongs deeply into the meat. Lock the forks in place with the screws, leaving at least 1 inch of free space on both ends of the rod.
5. Ensure the drip tray is in the bottom of the unit.
6. Guide the spit into the rotisserie position by placing the left shaft into the rotisserie gear located on the left interior wall. Once in place, lift and lay the right shaft on the rotisserie holder located on the right interior wall. Be sure that the lamb can rotate freely in the air fryer. Close the door.
7. Select the AIR FRY function, choose the MEAT icon, set the temperature to 375°F, and the time to 1 hour 30 minutes. Press the ROTATE button.
8. Press the START button to begin cooking.
9. Once cooking is complete and the internal temperature reaches 145°F (medium-rare), carefully remove the lamb using the fetch tool and let it rest for 15 minutes before slicing.
10. Serve warm.

Lemon Herb Lamb Chops with Roasted Bell Peppers

Serves: 4

|PREP TIME: 10 minutes
|COOK TIME: 15 minutes

For the Lamb Chops:
4 lamb chops
2 tbsps. olive oil
2 cloves garlic, minced
1 tbsp. lemon juice
1 tsp. lemon zest
1 tbsp. fresh parsley, chopped
½ tsp. salt

¼ tsp. black pepper
For the Bell Peppers:
2 red bell peppers, cut into strips
2 tbsps. olive oil
1 tsp. garlic powder
½ tsp. salt
¼ tsp. black pepper

For the Lamb Chops:
1. In a small bowl, mix the olive oil, minced garlic, lemon juice, lemon zest, parsley, salt, and black pepper.
2. Rub the mixture all over the lamb chops.
3. Lightly grease one wire rack.
4. Arrange the lamb chops on the wire rack in a single layer.
For the Bell Peppers:
5. In a large bowl, toss the bell pepper strips with olive oil, garlic powder, salt, and black pepper until evenly coated.
6. Lightly grease another wire rack.
7. Spread the bell peppers evenly on the wire rack.
8. Position the drip tray on the floor of the unit for easy cleaning.
9. Insert the wire racks with lamb chops and bell peppers into the Air Fryer. Close the door.
10. Select the AIR FRY function, set the temperature to 375°F, and the time to 15 minutes. Press the START button to begin cooking.
11. Halfway through the cooking time, switch the rack positions from top to bottom to ensure even cooking.
12. Once the lamb chops are cooked to your desired doneness and the bell peppers are tender and slightly charred, remove them from the Air Fryer.
13. Serve warm.

Pomegranate Glazed Lamb Ribs

Serves: 4

|PREP TIME: 15 minutes
|COOK TIME: 25 minutes

2 lbs. lamb ribs
¼ cup pomegranate molasses
2 tbsps. honey
2 cloves garlic, minced
1 tsp. ground cinnamon
½ tsp. salt
½ tsp. black pepper

1. In a small bowl, mix the pomegranate molasses, honey, minced garlic, ground cinnamon, salt, and black pepper.
2. Rub the mixture all over the lamb ribs.
3. Lightly grease one wire rack.
4. Arrange the lamb ribs on the wire rack in a single layer.
5. Position the drip tray on the floor of the unit for easy cleaning.
6. Insert the wire rack into the Air Fryer. Close the door.
7. Select the AIR FRY function, choose the MEAT icon, set the temperature to 375°F, and the time to 25 minutes. Press the START button to begin cooking.
8. Halfway through the cooking time, flip the lamb ribs to ensure even cooking.
9. Once the lamb ribs are cooked to your desired doneness and caramelized, remove them from the Air Fryer.
10. Serve warm.

Lamb and Mushroom Skewers

Serves: 4

1 lb. lamb leg, cut into 1-inch cubes
8 oz. button mushrooms, halved
¼ cup olive oil
2 cloves garlic, minced
1 tsp. dried rosemary
1 tsp. dried thyme
½ tsp. salt
¼ tsp. black pepper

|PREP TIME: 15 minutes
|COOK TIME: 12 minutes

1. In a large bowl, mix the olive oil, minced garlic, rosemary, thyme, salt, and black pepper.
2. Add the lamb cubes and mushroom halves to the mixture and toss until evenly coated.
3. Thread the marinated lamb and mushrooms onto skewers.
4. Lightly grease one wire rack.
5. Arrange the lamb and mushroom skewers on the wire rack.
6. Position the drip tray on the floor of the unit for easy cleaning.
7. Insert the wire rack into the Air Fryer. Close the door.
8. Select the AIR FRY function, choose the MEAT icon, set the temperature to 390°F, and the time to 12 minutes. Press the START button to begin cooking.
9. Halfway through the cooking time, flip the skewers to ensure even cooking.
10. Once the lamb is cooked through and the mushrooms are tender, remove the skewers from the Air Fryer.
11. Serve warm.

Herbed Lamb and Baby Potatoes

Serves: 4

1½ lbs. lamb shoulder, cut into 1-inch cubes
1 lb. baby potatoes, halved
¼ cup olive oil
2 cloves garlic, minced
1 tbsp. dried rosemary
1 tbsp. dried thyme
½ tsp. salt
½ tsp. black pepper

|PREP TIME: 15 minutes
|COOK TIME: 25 minutes

1. In a large bowl, mix the olive oil, minced garlic, rosemary, thyme, salt, and black pepper.
2. Add the lamb cubes and baby potatoes to the mixture and toss until evenly coated.
3. Lightly grease two wire racks.
4. Spread the lamb cubes on one wire rack and the baby potatoes on another wire rack.
5. Position the drip tray on the floor of the unit for easy cleaning.
6. Insert the wire racks into the Air Fryer. Close the door.
7. Select the AIR FRY function, set the temperature to 375°F, and the time to 25 minutes. Press the START button to begin cooking.
8. Halfway through the cooking time, switch the rack positions from top to bottom to ensure even cooking. Toss the lamb and potatoes if desired.
9. Once the lamb is cooked through and the potatoes are crispy and golden, remove them from the Air Fryer.
10. Serve warm.

CHAPTER 9

Snack and
Dehydrated Foods

Paprika Sweet Potato Fries

Serves: 4

3 large sweet potatoes, peeled and cut into fries
2 tbsps. olive oil
1 tsp. paprika
½ tsp. garlic powder
½ tsp. salt
¼ tsp. black pepper

|PREP TIME: 10 minutes
|COOK TIME: 18 minutes

1. In a large bowl, toss the sweet potato fries with olive oil, paprika, garlic powder, salt, and black pepper until evenly coated.
2. Lightly grease two wire racks.
3. Spread the sweet potato fries evenly on the wire racks.
4. Position the drip tray on the floor of the unit for easy cleaning.
5. Insert the wire racks into the Air Fryer. Close the door.
6. Select the AIR FRY function, choose the FRIES icon, set the temperature to 400°F, and the time to 18 minutes. Press the START button to begin cooking.
7. Halfway through the cooking time, switch the rack positions from top to bottom to ensure even cooking.
8. Once the fries are golden brown and crispy, remove them from the Air Fryer.
9. Serve warm.

Spiced Apple Chips

Serves: 4-6

4 apples, sliced into ¼-inch rings
1 tsp. ground cinnamon
½ tsp. ground nutmeg
1 tbsp. lemon juice

|PREP TIME: 10 minutes
|COOK TIME: 6 hours

1. Mix the apple slices with lemon juice, cinnamon, and nutmeg in a large bowl until evenly coated.
2. Arrange the apple slices on the wire racks, ensuring they do not overlap.
3. Position the drip tray on the floor of the unit for easy cleaning.
4. Insert the wire racks into the Air Fryer. Close the door.
5. Select the DEHYDRATE function. Choose the FRUIT icon, set the temperature to 135°F and the time to 6 hours.
6. Press the START button to begin dehydration.
7. Halfway through the dehydration process, open the air fryer door and switch the rack positions from top to bottom for even drying.
8. After 6 hours, check the apple chips for dryness. If they are not completely dry, add additional time in 30-minute increments until they reach the desired texture.
9. Remove the apple chips from the air fryer and let them cool completely.
10. Store in an airtight container at room temperature for up to 2 weeks.

Rotisserie Spiced Pineapple

Serves: 4

|PREP TIME: 10 minutes
|COOK TIME: 45 minutes

1 whole pineapple, peeled and cored
2 tbsps. honey
1 tbsp. lime juice
1 tsp. ground cinnamon
½ tsp. ground nutmeg
¼ tsp. ground cloves

1. In a small bowl, mix together honey, lime juice, cinnamon, nutmeg, and cloves.
2. Brush the spiced honey mixture all over the pineapple, ensuring it is evenly coated.
3. Secure the pineapple on the rotisserie spit, ensuring it is balanced. Carefully slide the spit forks onto the shaft on both ends of the pineapple. Lock the forks in place with the screws, leaving at least 1 inch of free space on both ends of the rod.
4. Ensure the drip tray is in the bottom of the unit.
5. Guide the spit into the rotisserie position by placing the left shaft into the rotisserie gear located on the left interior wall. Once in place, lift and lay the right shaft on the rotisserie holder located on the right interior wall. Be sure that the pineapple can rotate freely in the air fryer. Close the door.
6. Select the AIR FRY function, choose the FRUIT icon, set the temperature to 375°F, and the time to 45 minutes. Press the ROTATE button.
7. Press the START button to begin cooking.
8. Once cooking is complete, carefully remove the pineapple using the fetch tool.
9. Let the pineapple cool slightly before slicing into rings.
10. Serve warm or at room temperature.

Sweet Pear Slices

Serves: 4

|PREP TIME: 10 minutes
|COOK TIME: 6 hours

4 ripe pears, sliced into ¼-inch pieces
2 tbsps. lemon juice
1 tbsp. honey

1. Mix the pear slices with lemon juice and honey in a large bowl until evenly coated.
2. Arrange the pear slices on the wire racks, ensuring they do not overlap.
3. Position the drip tray on the floor of the unit for easy cleaning.
4. Insert the wire racks into the Air Fryer. Close the door.
5. Select the DEHYDRATE function. Choose the FRUIT icon, set the temperature to 135°F and the time to 6 hours.
6. Press the START button to begin dehydration.
7. Halfway through the dehydration process, open the air fryer door and switch the rack positions from top to bottom for even drying.
8. After 6 hours, check the pear slices for dryness. If they are not completely dry, add additional time in 30-minute increments until they reach the desired texture.
9. Remove the pear slices from the air fryer and let them cool completely.
10. Store in an airtight container at room temperature for up to 2 weeks.

Zucchini Chips & Mini Meatballs

Serves: 4

For the Zucchini Chips:
2 medium zucchinis, thinly sliced
2 tbsps. olive oil
½ tsp. garlic powder
½ tsp. paprika
½ tsp. salt
¼ tsp. black pepper
For the Mini Meatballs:
1 lb. ground beef

¼ cup bread crumbs
¼ cup grated Parmesan cheese
1 egg
2 garlic cloves, minced
1 tsp. Italian seasoning
½ tsp. salt
¼ tsp. black pepper
Marinara sauce for serving

|PREP TIME: 20 minutes
|COOK TIME: 15 minutes

For the Zucchini Chips:
1. In a large bowl, toss zucchini slices with olive oil, garlic powder, paprika, salt, and black pepper until evenly coated.
2. Spread the zucchini slices evenly on one greased wire rack.

For the Mini Meatballs:
3. In a large bowl, combine ground beef, bread crumbs, grated Parmesan cheese, egg, minced garlic, Italian seasoning, salt, and black pepper.
4. Mix until well combined and form into small meatballs.
5. Place the mini meatballs on the second wire rack.
6. Position the drip tray on the floor of the unit for easy cleaning.
7. Insert both wire racks into the Air Fryer. Close the door.
8. Select the AIR FRY function, set the temperature to 375°F, and the time to 15 minutes. Press the START button to begin cooking.
9. Halfway through the cooking time, switch the rack positions from top to bottom to ensure even cooking.
10. Once the zucchini chips are crispy and the mini meatballs are cooked through and browned, remove them from the Air Fryer.
11. Serve the zucchini chips with a dipping sauce of your choice and the mini meatballs with marinara sauce.

Crispy Beet Chips

Serves: 6

3 large beets, sliced into ⅛-inch pieces
2 tbsps. olive oil
½ tsp. sea salt

|PREP TIME: 10 minutes
|COOK TIME: 10 hours

1. Mix the beet slices with olive oil and sea salt in a large bowl until evenly coated.
2. Arrange the beet slices on the wire racks, ensuring they do not overlap.
3. Position the drip tray on the floor of the unit for easy cleaning.
4. Insert the wire racks into the Air Fryer. Close the door.
5. Select the DEHYDRATE function. Choose the VEGETABLES icon, set the temperature to 135°F and the time to 10 hours.
6. Press the START button to begin dehydration.
7. Halfway through the dehydration process, open the air fryer door and switch the rack positions from top to bottom for even drying.
8. After 10 hours, check the beet chips for dryness. If they are not completely dry, add additional time in 30-minute increments until they reach the desired texture.
9. Remove the beet chips from the air fryer and let them cool completely.
10. Store in an airtight container at room temperature for up to 2 weeks.

Mozzarella Sticks

Serves: 4

|PREP TIME: 10 minutes
|COOK TIME: 10 minutes

12 mozzarella sticks
1 cup flour
2 eggs, beaten
1 cup bread crumbs
½ tsp. garlic powder
½ tsp. Italian seasoning
Marinara sauce for serving

1. Set up a breading station with three shallow bowls: one with flour, one with beaten eggs, and one with a mixture of bread crumbs, garlic powder, and Italian seasoning.
2. Coat each mozzarella stick in flour, then dip in beaten eggs, and finally coat with the bread crumb mixture.
3. Lightly grease one wire rack.
4. Arrange the breaded mozzarella sticks on the wire rack.
5. Position the drip tray on the floor of the unit for easy cleaning.
6. Insert the wire rack into the Air Fryer. Close the door.
7. Select the AIR FRY function, set the temperature to 375°F, and the time to 10 minutes. Press the START button to begin cooking.
8. Once the mozzarella sticks are golden brown and crispy, remove them from the Air Fryer.
9. Serve warm with marinara sauce.

Zesty Orange Slices

Serves: 4

|PREP TIME: 10 minutes
|COOK TIME: 6 hours

4 oranges, sliced into ¼-inch rounds
1 tbsp. lemon juice
1 tbsp. sugar

1. Mix the orange slices with lemon juice and sugar in a large bowl until evenly coated.
2. Arrange the orange slices on the wire racks, ensuring they do not overlap.
3. Position the drip tray on the floor of the unit for easy cleaning.
4. Insert the wire racks into the Air Fryer. Close the door.
5. Select the DEHYDRATE function. Choose the FRUIT icon, set the temperature to 135°F and the time to 6 hours.
6. Press the START button to begin dehydration.
7. Halfway through the dehydration process, open the air fryer door and switch the rack positions from top to bottom for even drying.
8. After 6 hours, check the orange slices for dryness. If they are not completely dry, add additional time in 30-minute increments until they reach the desired texture.
9. Remove the orange slices from the air fryer and let them cool completely.
10. Store in an airtight container at room temperature for up to 2 weeks.

Cheese Stuffed Jalapeños

Serves: 6

12 large jalapeños, halved and seeded
8 oz. cream cheese, softened
1 cup shredded cheddar cheese
½ tsp. garlic powder
½ tsp. onion powder
¼ tsp. salt

|PREP TIME: 10 minutes
|COOK TIME: 10 minutes

1. In a bowl, mix together the cream cheese, shredded cheddar cheese, garlic powder, onion powder, and salt.
2. Fill each jalapeño half with the cheese mixture.
3. Lightly grease the wire racks.
4. Arrange the stuffed jalapeños on the wire racks.
5. Position the drip tray on the floor of the unit for easy cleaning.
6. Insert the wire racks into the Air Fryer. Close the door.
7. Select the AIR FRY function, choose the VEGETABLES icon, set the temperature to 375°F, and the time to 10 minutes. Press the START button to begin cooking.
8. Halfway through the cooking time, switch the rack positions from top to bottom to ensure even cooking.
9. Once the jalapeños are tender and the cheese is melted and bubbly, remove them from the Air Fryer.
10. Serve warm.

Spiced Tomato Chips

Serves: 6

6 large tomatoes, sliced into ⅛-inch pieces
2 tbsps. olive oil
1 tsp. dried basil
1 tsp. sea salt

|PREP TIME: 10 minutes
|COOK TIME: 10 hours

1. Mix the tomato slices with olive oil, basil, and sea salt in a large bowl until evenly coated.
2. Arrange the tomato slices on the wire racks, ensuring they do not overlap.
3. Position the drip tray on the floor of the unit for easy cleaning.
4. Insert the wire racks into the Air Fryer. Close the door.
5. Select the DEHYDRATE function. Choose the VEGETABLES icon, set the temperature to 125°F and the time to 10 hours.
6. Press the START button to begin dehydration.
7. Halfway through the dehydration process, open the air fryer door and switch the rack positions from top to bottom for even drying.
8. After 10 hours, check the tomato chips for dryness. If they are not completely dry, add additional time in 30-minute increments until they reach the desired texture.
9. Remove the tomato chips from the air fryer and let them cool completely.
10. Store in an airtight container at room temperature for up to 2 weeks.

Tangy Mango Slices

Serves: 6

|PREP TIME: 10 minutes
|COOK TIME: 8 hours

4 ripe mangoes, sliced into ¼-inch pieces
2 tbsps. lime juice
1 tbsp. honey

1. Mix the mango slices with lime juice and honey in a large bowl until evenly coated.
2. Arrange the mango slices on the wire racks, ensuring they do not overlap.
3. Position the drip tray on the floor of the unit for easy cleaning.
4. Insert the wire racks into the Air Fryer. Close the door.
5. Select the DEHYDRATE function. Choose the FRUIT icon, set the temperature to 135°F and the time to 8 hours.
6. Press the START button to begin dehydration.
7. Halfway through the dehydration process, open the air fryer door and switch the rack positions from top to bottom for even drying.
8. After 8 hours, check the mango slices for dryness. If they are not completely dry, add additional time in 30-minute increments until they reach the desired texture.
9. Remove the mango slices from the air fryer and let them cool completely.
10. Store in an airtight container at room temperature for up to 2 weeks.

Garlic Parmesan Wings

Serves: 4

|PREP TIME: 10 minutes
|COOK TIME: 25 minutes

2 lbs. chicken wings
2 tbsps. olive oil
1 tsp. garlic powder
½ tsp. salt
½ tsp. black pepper
¼ cup grated Parmesan cheese
2 tbsps. chopped fresh parsley (optional)

1. In a large bowl, toss the chicken wings with olive oil, garlic powder, salt, and black pepper until evenly coated.
2. Lightly grease two wire racks.
3. Arrange the chicken wings on the wire racks in a single layer, ensuring they do not overlap.
4. Position the drip tray on the floor of the unit for easy cleaning.
5. Insert the wire racks into the Air Fryer. Close the door.
6. Select the AIR FRY function, choose the CHICKEN icon, set the temperature to 375°F, and the time to 25 minutes. Press the START button to begin cooking.
7. Halfway through the cooking time, switch the rack positions from top to bottom to ensure even cooking.
8. Once the wings are golden brown and crispy, remove them from the Air Fryer.
9. Toss the wings with grated Parmesan cheese and chopped fresh parsley if desired.
10. Serve warm.

Crispy Onion Rings

Serves: 4

2 large onions, sliced into rings
1 cup flour
2 eggs, beaten
1 cup bread crumbs
½ tsp. salt
½ tsp. black pepper
½ tsp. paprika
Ketchup for serving

|PREP TIME: 10 minutes
|COOK TIME: 12 minutes

1. Set up a breading station with three shallow bowls: one with flour, one with beaten eggs, and one with a mixture of bread crumbs, salt, black pepper, and paprika.
2. Coat each onion ring in flour, then dip in beaten eggs, and finally coat with the bread crumb mixture.
3. Lightly grease two wire racks.
4. Arrange the breaded onion rings on the wire racks.
5. Position the drip tray on the floor of the unit for easy cleaning.
6. Insert the wire racks into the Air Fryer. Close the door.
7. Select the AIR FRY function, choose the VEGETABLES icon, set the temperature to 375°F, and the time to 12 minutes. Press the START button to begin cooking.
8. Halfway through the cooking time, switch the rack positions from top to bottom to ensure even cooking.
9. Once the onion rings are golden brown and crispy, remove them from the Air Fryer.
10. Serve warm with ketchup.

Savory Kale Chips

Serves: 4-6

1 large bunch of kale, stems removed and torn into ¼-inch pieces
2 tbsps. olive oil
1 tsp. garlic powder
½ tsp. sea salt

|PREP TIME: 10 minutes
|COOK TIME: 4 hours

1. Mix the kale pieces with olive oil, garlic powder, and sea salt in a large bowl until evenly coated.
2. Arrange the kale pieces on the wire racks, ensuring they do not overlap.
3. Position the drip tray on the floor of the unit for easy cleaning.
4. Insert the wire racks into the Air Fryer. Close the door.
5. Select the DEHYDRATE function. Choose the VEGETABLES icon, set the temperature to 125°F and the time to 4 hours.
6. Press the START button to begin dehydration.
7. Halfway through the dehydration process, open the air fryer door and switch the rack positions from top to bottom for even drying.
8. After 4 hours, check the kale chips for dryness. If they are not completely dry, add additional time in 30-minute increments until they reach the desired texture.
9. Remove the kale chips from the air fryer and let them cool completely.
10. Store in an airtight container at room temperature for up to 2 weeks.

CHAPTER 10
Dessert

Homemade Brownies

Serves: 16

½ cup unsalted butter, melted
1 cup granulated sugar
2 large eggs
1 tsp. vanilla extract
⅓ cup unsweetened cocoa powder
½ cup all-purpose flour
¼ tsp. salt
¼ tsp. baking powder

|PREP TIME: 10 minutes
|COOK TIME: 20 minutes

1. In a medium bowl, mix together the melted butter, sugar, eggs, and vanilla extract.
2. Add the cocoa powder, flour, salt, and baking powder. Stir until well blended.
3. Spread the batter evenly in a lightly greased baking pan that fits into your air fryer.
4. Place the baking pan on the drip tray and insert the tray into the Air Fryer. Close the door.
5. Select the BAKE function, choose the CAKE icon, set the temperature to 350°F, and the time to 20 minutes. Press the START button to begin cooking.
6. Bake until a toothpick inserted into the center comes out clean.
7. Let the brownies cool in the pan before cutting into squares.
8. Serve and enjoy.

Cinnamon Sugar Donuts

Serves: 12 donuts

1 can refrigerated biscuit dough (10-12 biscuits)
½ cup granulated sugar
1 tsp. ground cinnamon
¼ cup melted butter

|PREP TIME: 15 minutes
|COOK TIME: 10 minutes

1. In a small bowl, mix together the granulated sugar and ground cinnamon.
2. Cut the center out of each biscuit to form a donut shape.
3. Lightly grease two wire racks.
4. Arrange the donuts and donut holes on the wire racks in a single layer.
5. Position the drip tray on the floor of the unit for easy cleaning.
6. Insert the wire racks into the Air Fryer. Close the door.
7. Select the AIR FRY function, set the temperature to 350°F, and the time to 10 minutes. Press the START button to begin cooking.
8. Halfway through the cooking time, switch the rack positions from top to bottom to ensure even cooking.
9. Once the donuts are golden brown, remove them from the Air Fryer.
10. While the donuts are still warm, brush them with melted butter and coat with the cinnamon-sugar mixture.
11. Serve warm.

Tasty Lemon Bars

Serves: 16

|PREP TIME: 15 minutes
|COOK TIME: 20 minutes

1 cup all-purpose flour
½ cup powdered sugar
½ cup unsalted butter, softened
1 cup granulated sugar
2 large eggs
½ cup lemon juice
2 tbsps. all-purpose flour
½ tsp. baking powder
Powdered sugar for dusting

1. In a medium bowl, mix 1 cup flour and ½ cup powdered sugar. Cut in the butter until the mixture resembles coarse crumbs.
2. Press the mixture into a lightly greased baking pan that fits into your air fryer.
3. Place the baking pan on the drip tray and insert the tray into the Air Fryer. Close the door.
4. Select the BAKE function, set the temperature to 350°F, and the time to 20 minutes. Press the START button to begin cooking.
5. While the crust is baking, whisk together the granulated sugar, eggs, lemon juice, 2 tbsps. flour, and baking powder until smooth.
6. After 10 minutes, pour the lemon mixture over the partially baked crust. Press the START button to continue cooking.
7. Bake until the lemon filling is set.
8. Let the lemon bars cool in the pan before dusting with powdered sugar and cutting into squares.
9. Serve and enjoy.

Cheesecake Bites

Serves: 24 bites

|PREP TIME: 20 minutes
|COOK TIME: 12 minutes

1 cup graham cracker crumbs
3 tbsps. melted butter
16 oz. cream cheese, softened
½ cup granulated sugar
2 large eggs
1 tsp. vanilla extract

1. In a medium bowl, combine graham cracker crumbs and melted butter. Press into the bottom of mini muffin cups.
2. In a large bowl, beat cream cheese and sugar until smooth. Add eggs and vanilla extract, beating until well combined.
3. Spoon the cream cheese mixture over the graham cracker crusts in the mini muffin cups.
4. Lightly grease the wire racks.
5. Arrange the mini muffin cups on the wire racks.
6. Position the drip tray on the floor of the unit for easy cleaning.
7. Insert the wire racks into the Air Fryer. Close the door.
8. Select the BAKE function, choose the CAKE icon, set the temperature to 325°F, and the time to 12 minutes. Press the START button to begin cooking.
9. Halfway through the cooking time, switch the rack positions from top to bottom to ensure even cooking.
10. Once the cheesecake bites are set, remove them from the Air Fryer and let them cool completely.
11. Serve chilled.

Healthy Pumpkin Bread

Serves: 8

1¾ cups all-purpose flour
1 cup granulated sugar
½ cup brown sugar
1 tsp. baking soda
½ tsp. salt
½ tsp. ground cinnamon
½ tsp. ground nutmeg
¼ tsp. ground cloves
¼ tsp. ground ginger
2 large eggs
1 cup canned pumpkin puree
½ cup vegetable oil
⅓ cup water
1 tsp. vanilla extract

|PREP TIME: 15 minutes
|COOK TIME: 30 minutes

1. In a large bowl, whisk together the flour, granulated sugar, brown sugar, baking soda, salt, cinnamon, nutmeg, cloves, and ginger.
2. In another bowl, mix together the eggs, pumpkin puree, vegetable oil, water, and vanilla extract.
3. Pour the wet ingredients into the dry ingredients and mix until just combined.
4. Lightly grease a loaf pan that fits into your air fryer.
5. Pour the batter into the prepared loaf pan.
6. Place the loaf pan on the drip tray and insert the tray into the Air Fryer. Close the door.
7. Select the BAKE function, choose the CAKE icon, set the temperature to 350°F, and the time to 30 minutes. Press the START button to begin cooking.
8. Bake until a toothpick inserted into the center comes out clean.
9. Let the pumpkin bread cool in the pan before slicing and serving.

Chocolate Lava Cakes

Serves: 4

½ cup unsalted butter
4 oz. semi-sweet chocolate, chopped
1 cup powdered sugar
2 large eggs
2 large egg yolks
1 tsp. vanilla extract
½ cup all-purpose flour

|PREP TIME: 15 minutes
|COOK TIME: 12 minutes

1. In a microwave-safe bowl, melt the butter and semi-sweet chocolate together until smooth.
2. Stir in the powdered sugar until well combined.
3. Add the eggs and egg yolks, then mix in the vanilla extract.
4. Stir in the flour until just combined.
5. Lightly grease four ramekins that fit into your air fryer.
6. Divide the batter evenly among the prepared ramekins.
7. Place the ramekins on the drip tray and insert the tray into the Air Fryer. Close the door.
8. Select the BAKE function, choose the CAKE icon, set the temperature to 375°F, and the time to 12 minutes. Press the START button to begin cooking.
9. Bake until the edges are set, but the center is still soft.
10. Let the lava cakes cool in the ramekins for a few minutes before inverting onto plates.
11. Serve warm with ice cream or whipped cream.

Peanut Butter Cookies

|PREP TIME: 10 minutes
|COOK TIME: 12 minutes

1 cup unsalted butter, softened
1 cup granulated sugar
1 cup brown sugar
1 cup peanut butter
2 large eggs
2½ cups all-purpose flour
1 tsp. baking soda
½ tsp. baking powder
½ tsp. salt

1. In a large bowl, cream together the butter, granulated sugar, brown sugar, and peanut butter until smooth.
2. Beat in the eggs one at a time.
3. Combine the flour, baking soda, baking powder, and salt; gradually blend into the creamed mixture.
4. Roll the dough into 1-inch balls and place on lightly greased wire racks.
5. Flatten each ball with a fork, making a criss-cross pattern.
6. Position the drip tray on the floor of the unit for easy cleaning.
7. Insert the wire racks into the Air Fryer. Close the door.
8. Select the BAKE function, set the temperature to 350°F, and the time to 12 minutes. Press the START button to begin cooking.
9. Halfway through the cooking time, switch the rack positions from top to bottom to ensure even cooking.
10. Once the cookies are golden brown, remove them from the Air Fryer.
11. Let the cookies cool on the wire racks before serving.

Carrot Cake Muffins

|PREP TIME: 15 minutes
|COOK TIME: 18 minutes

1½ cups all-purpose flour
1 tsp. baking powder
½ tsp. baking soda
½ tsp. salt
1 tsp. ground cinnamon
½ tsp. ground nutmeg
½ cup vegetable oil

½ cup granulated sugar
½ cup brown sugar
2 large eggs
1 tsp. vanilla extract
1½ cups grated carrots
½ cup chopped walnuts (optional)

1. In a large bowl, whisk together the flour, baking powder, baking soda, salt, cinnamon, and nutmeg.
2. In another bowl, beat together the oil, granulated sugar, and brown sugar until well combined.
3. Add the eggs and vanilla extract, beating until smooth.
4. Gradually add the dry ingredients to the wet ingredients, mixing until just combined.
5. Fold in the grated carrots and chopped walnuts, if using.
6. Lightly grease a muffin pan that fits into your air fryer.
7. Divide the batter evenly among the muffin cups.
8. Place the muffin pan on the drip tray and insert the tray into the Air Fryer. Close the door.
9. Select the BAKE function, choose the CAKE icon, set the temperature to 350°F, and the time to 18 minutes. Press the START button to begin cooking.
10. Bake until a toothpick inserted into the center comes out clean.
11. Let the muffins cool in the pan before serving.

Easy Berry Crumble

Serves: 4

2 cups mixed berries (strawberries, blueberries, raspberries)
¼ cup granulated sugar
1 tbsp. cornstarch
½ cup all-purpose flour
½ cup rolled oats
¼ cup brown sugar
¼ cup unsalted butter, melted
½ tsp. cinnamon

|PREP TIME: 10 minutes
|COOK TIME: 20 minutes

1. In a medium bowl, combine the mixed berries, granulated sugar, and cornstarch. Pour into a baking dish that fits into your air fryer.
2. In another bowl, mix together the flour, rolled oats, brown sugar, melted butter, and cinnamon until crumbly.
3. Sprinkle the crumble mixture evenly over the berries.
4. Place the baking dish on the drip tray and insert the tray into the Air Fryer. Close the door.
5. Select the BAKE function, set the temperature to 350°F, and the time to 20 minutes. Press the START button to begin cooking.
6. Once the crumble is golden brown and the berries are bubbling, remove it from the Air Fryer.
7. Serve warm with ice cream or whipped cream.

Classic Churros

Serves: 4

1 cup water
2½ tbsps. granulated sugar
½ tsp. salt
2 tbsps. vegetable oil
1 cup all-purpose flour
½ cup granulated sugar
1 tsp. ground cinnamon

|PREP TIME: 15 minutes
|COOK TIME: 10 minutes

1. In a small saucepan over medium heat, combine water, 2½ tbsps. sugar, salt, and vegetable oil. Bring to a boil and remove from heat.
2. Stir in the flour until the mixture forms a ball.
3. Spoon the dough into a piping bag fitted with a large star tip.
4. Lightly grease two wire racks.
5. Pipe strips of dough onto the wire racks.
6. Position the drip tray on the floor of the unit for easy cleaning.
7. Insert the wire racks into the Air Fryer. Close the door.
8. Select the AIR FRY function, set the temperature to 375°F, and the time to 10 minutes. Press the START button to begin cooking.
9. Halfway through the cooking time, switch the rack positions from top to bottom to ensure even cooking.
10. In a shallow dish, mix ½ cup sugar and ground cinnamon.
11. Once the churros are golden brown, remove them from the Air Fryer and roll them in the cinnamon-sugar mixture.
12. Serve warm.

Peach Cobbler

Serves: 6

|PREP TIME: 15 minutes
|COOK TIME: 20 minutes

4 cups sliced peaches (fresh or frozen, thawed)
¼ cup granulated sugar
1 tsp. lemon juice
1 cup all-purpose flour
1 cup granulated sugar
1 tsp. baking powder
¼ tsp. salt
½ cup unsalted butter, melted
1 cup milk

1. In a bowl, combine the sliced peaches, ¼ cup granulated sugar, and lemon juice.
2. In another bowl, mix together the flour, 1 cup granulated sugar, baking powder, and salt. Add the melted butter and milk, stirring until well combined.
3. Pour the batter into a lightly greased baking dish that fits into your air fryer.
4. Spoon the peach mixture evenly over the batter.
5. Place the baking dish on the drip tray and insert the tray into the Air Fryer. Close the door.
6. Select the BAKE function, set the temperature to 350°F, and the time to 20 minutes. Press the START button to begin cooking.
7. Once the cobbler is golden brown and the peaches are tender, remove it from the Air Fryer.
8. Serve warm with vanilla ice cream or whipped cream.

Coconut Macaroons

Serves: 20

|PREP TIME: 10 minutes
|COOK TIME: 12 minutes

2½ cups sweetened shredded coconut
½ cup sweetened condensed milk
1 tsp. vanilla extract
2 large egg whites
¼ tsp. salt
½ cup semi-sweet chocolate chips (optional, for drizzling)

1. In a large bowl, combine the shredded coconut, sweetened condensed milk, and vanilla extract.
2. In another bowl, beat the egg whites and salt until stiff peaks form.
3. Gently fold the egg whites into the coconut mixture until well combined.
4. Drop spoonfuls of the mixture onto a lightly greased wire rack, forming small mounds.
5. Position the drip tray on the floor of the unit for easy cleaning.
6. Insert the wire rack into the Air Fryer. Close the door.
7. Select the BAKE function, set the temperature to 325°F, and the time to 12 minutes. Press the START button to begin cooking.
8. Once the macaroons are golden brown, remove them from the Air Fryer and let them cool.
9. If desired, melt the chocolate chips in the microwave and drizzle over the cooled macaroons.
10. Serve and enjoy.

Appendix 1: Basic Kitchen Conversions & Equivalents

DRY MEASUREMENTS CONVERSION CHART

3 teaspoons = 1 tablespoon = 1/16 cup
6 teaspoons = 2 tablespoons = 1/8 cup
12 teaspoons = 4 tablespoons = ¼ cup
24 teaspoons = 8 tablespoons = ½ cup
36 teaspoons = 12 tablespoons = ¾ cup
48 teaspoons = 16 tablespoons = 1 cup

METRIC TO US COOKING CONVERSIONS

OVEN TEMPERATURES

120 °C = 250 °F
160 °C = 320 °F
180 °C = 350 °F
205 °C = 400 °F
220 °C = 425 °F

LIQUID MEASUREMENTS CONVERSION CHART

8 fluid ounces = 1 cup = ½ pint = ¼ quart
16 fluid ounces = 2 cups = 1 pint = ½ quart
32 fluid ounces = 4 cups = 2 pints = 1 quart = ¼ gallon
128 fluid ounces = 16 cups = 8 pints = 4 quarts = 1 gallon

BAKING IN GRAMS

1 cup flour = 140 grams
1 cup sugar = 150 grams
1 cup powdered sugar = 160 grams
1 cup heavy cream = 235 grams

VOLUME

1 milliliter = 1/5 teaspoon
5 ml = 1 teaspoon
15 ml = 1 tablespoon
240 ml = 1 cup or 8 fluid ounces
1 liter = 34 fluid ounces

WEIGHT

1 gram = .035 ounces
100 grams = 3.5 ounces
500 grams = 1.1 pounds
1 kilogram = 35 ounces

US TO METRIC COOKING CONVERSIONS

1/5 tsp = 1 ml
1 tsp = 5 ml
1 tbsp = 15 ml
1 fluid ounces = 30 ml
1 cup = 237 ml
1 pint (2 cups) = 473 ml
1 quart (4 cups) = .95 liter
1 gallon (16 cups) = 3.8 liters
1 oz = 28 grams
1 pound = 454 grams

BUTTER

1 cup butter = 2 sticks = 8 ounces = 230 grams = 16 tablespoons

WHAT DOES 1 CUP EQUAL

1 cup = 8 fluid ounces
1 cup = 16 tablespoons
1 cup = 48 teaspoons
1 cup = ½ pint
1 cup = ¼ quart
1 cup = 1/16 gallon
1 cup = 240 ml

BAKING PAN CONVERSIONS

9-inch round cake pan = 12 cups
10-inch tube pan =16 cups
10-inch bundt pan = 12 cups
9-inch springform pan = 10 cups
9 x 5 inch loaf pan = 8 cups
9-inch square pan = 8 cups

BAKING PAN CONVERSIONS

1 cup all-purpose flour = 4.5 oz
1 cup rolled oats = 3 oz
1 large egg = 1.7 oz
1 cup butter = 8 oz
1 cup milk = 8 oz
1 cup heavy cream = 8.4 oz
1 cup granulated sugar = 7.1 oz
1 cup packed brown sugar = 7.75 oz
1 cup vegetable oil = 7.7 oz
1 cup unsifted powdered sugar = 4.4 oz

Appendix 2: CHEFMAN Air Fryer+ Preset Settings

AIR FRY Preset Settings

Preset	Default Time	Default Temp
Manual	15 min	400°F
Fries	20 min	400°F
Chicken	30 min	375°F
Fish	10 min	350°F
Meat	25 min	375°F
Vegetables	15 min	350°F

BAKE Preset Settings

Preset	Default Time	Default Temp
Manual	30 min	350°F
Cake	35 min	350°F
Chicken	45 min	375°F
Fish	15 min	350°F
Vegetables	25 min	350°F

DEHYDRATE Preset Settings

Preset	Default Time	Default Temp
Manual	10 hours	165°F
Chicken	6 hours	165°F
Fish	8 hours	165°F
Meat	6 hours	165°F
Vegetables	10 hours	125°F
Fruit	5 hours	135°F

NOTE: These are guidelines only; always check foods for doneness according to proper food safety guidelines.

Appendix 3: Recipes Index

Made in United States
Orlando, FL
06 December 2024